What Leaders Are Saying About

Leading from the Inside Out

"Marc Carignan has written a book whose time has come. The concepts are simple yet profoundly important to living an intentional life. If you are ready to create the financial, relational, intellectual, physical or spiritual wealth you deserve, then read this book!"

–JAMES MALINCHAK, co-author, *Chicken Soup for the Athlete's Soul*; co-author, *Chicken Soup for the College Soul*; two-time *College Speaker of the Year*; and featured expert & co-star of the blockbuster movie, *Pass It On*

"I worked with Marc. He's an exceptional leader. It's wonderful to see him set down his principles in writing and share them with aspiring leaders."

–MARTIN BRAUNS, retired chairman and CEO, Interwoven, Inc.

"*Leading from the Inside Out* is Positively Brilliant. When you are ready to claim your full power as a Positively Brilliant leader – buy this book. When you are ready to reconnect to all of your god-given talents, vision and purpose as a leader – devour this book and allow it to nurture your untapped capacity for *Leading from the Inside Out*."

–PETER J. REDING, author and visionary, of the *Positively Brilliant* series

"Marc provides over 20 different real-world practices that can change your life in a matter of weeks or even days. Two of the exercises alone, although amazingly simple, have totally transformed my life and the lives of my family members for the better. Life will never be the same. I love this guy and can't wait for his next book!"

–AJEET MIRWANI, keynote speaker, author, mentor

"*Leading from the Inside Out* is a powerful example of how deliberate intention can shape one's life. I recommend this book to corporate leaders, community organizers and those stepping into the power of personal leadership in their life. This is a must-read!"

– ELLEN WRIGHT-MONTGOMERY, president, Wright Consulting, Inc.

"What an inspirational book this is! Marc has done an amazing job of bringing together key leadership concepts with his unique perspective. If you are ready to connect to your 'inner leader' then read this book. A whole new level of clarity, joy and success awaits you."

– DON CAMPBELL, Silicon Valley entrepreneur

"Marc's leadership concepts are clear, powerful and easy to understand. Use the concepts presented within to be more effective at work, build a better life and have a lot more fun in the process!"

– KENDAL TEXEIRA, management consultant, life coach

"For those choosing to step into their own inner power, tapping into their inner leadership capabilities, you will get a new level of clarity by reading this book."

– JONATHAN SPRINKLES, motivational speaker and CEO, Sprinklisms

"This book will teach you how to work with The Laws that govern everything in this universe. For anyone who is ready to eliminate frustration and let their individual or organization's power unfold from within, this is a must read!"

– CHRIS J. SNOOK, international best-selling author of *Wealth Matters... Abundance is your birthright!*

LEADING FROM THE INSIDE OUT

7 STEPS TO INTENTIONALLY CREATE THE LIFE YOU DESIRE

MARC A. CARIGNAN

NEW LEADERS PUBLISHING
A DIVISION OF LIFE SUCCESS STRATEGIES INC.
SAN DIEGO, CALIFORNIA
WWW.LIFESUCCESSSTRATEGIES.COM

Published in the United States by New Leaders Publishing,
a division of Life Success Strategies Inc.

Life Success Strategies Inc.
1286 University Ave, Suite 700
San Diego, CA 92103 USA

Phone: 1-619-299-1700

Email: info@LifeSuccessStrategies.com

Internet: www.LifeSuccessStrategies.com

Carignan, Marc A.

LEADING FROM THE INSIDE OUT / 7 Steps to Intentionally Create the Life You Desire

ISBN: 978-0-9798649-0-2

Warning – Disclaimer

The purpose of this book is to educate and entertain. The author or publisher does not guarantee that anyone following the techniques, suggestions, tips, ideas, or strategies will become successful. The author and publisher shall have neither liability nor responsibility to anyone with respect to any loss or damage caused, or alleged to be caused, directly or indirectly by the information contained in this book.

Printed in the United States of America

First Edition

To Nicole, my sister and best friend,
with love and gratitude!

Contents

Introduction

If you aren't connected to nature's silent
effortless workings, what is the alternative?
Work, struggle, effort and frustration –
the very things we think are necessary
for any kind of great success.
– Deepak Chopra

Most of us think it's normal to work hard, struggle day in and day out, exert large amounts of effort and get frustrated along the way to our goals. Haven't you heard that you need to work hard for what you want? Doesn't struggle somehow seem heroic, that maybe if we are struggling then our goal is worthwhile? What if there is another way?

Each one of us is the creator of our own life experience. We have more influence over our successes than most people believe. Yet there seems to be a belief that if our lives were to get easier and we were to experience less struggle and more ease that we would just be getting lazy. What if you could deliberately choose your direction and at the same time move into the "flow" of ease, fun, joy and peace? It's time for a new way, where your outer world is created from, and a reflection of, your inner world.

The answer is in *Leading from the Inside Out*. It is about getting clear of your intentions, tapping into your inner strength and becoming more conscious about your place in the world. When you get clear, build habits that will support you, grow your confidence and develop a positive attitude, you become a deliberate and intentional leader of your life.

Why lead by intention? The benefits are many. They include living a life of real inner power, deep-felt passion, and abundant joy. The benefits also include achieving the financial goals you desire, creating the relationships you want, and building powerful habits that support your physical health and well-being.

This book provides seven powerful and clear steps to activate the power within you, the power of your "inner leader." To truly be successful, you must get clear about what you want in your life and then deliberately take the action to create it. In most cases, this is easier and even more fun than you may have imagined. When leading from the inside out, one taps into the power of intention. As opposed to traditional leadership approaches, leading by intention is not as much about discipline as it is about clarity and focus on your desires.

For new leaders developing their leadership styles, experienced leaders looking for new approaches, and for those who lead others in business and community settings, this book is an indispensable guide. In learning and living the principles of *Leading from the Inside Out*, you will have a much greater impact in influencing and inspiring others. When your thinking, feelings and actions are in alignment with your intentions, anything you choose can be yours.

You can accomplish anything in life, provided
that you do not mind who gets the credit.
– Harry S. Truman

This book is not about positive thinking. Although positive thinking is a good thing, it's only a beginning. This book is about being motivated and receiving inspiration from the "inside," causing your results to appear on the "outside." It's about simple yet powerful techniques to take hold of the creative power in your life. It's about redesigning the areas of your life that warrant it. It's about deciding what you really want and having the tools and techniques to pursue your dreams with confidence. It's about fully engaging in the "game of life" today, rather than hoping that someday you will get what you want to become happy. It's about trading in the idea of someday "arriving" at your goals and instead choosing joy and passion while pursuing them today.

Whatever your goals and whatever your desires, the principles, techniques and stories in this book will inspire, educate and instruct you to become a more deliberate creator in your own life. As you try out the ideas described in the book and put them into practice, you will be amazed at the rapid and dramatic changes you will experience in your life.

Provided within are keys to living a joyful life and having the things you truly desire. These concepts have worked for me and for countless others. Let's begin our journey together.

About Marc Carignan

Marc Carignan, President and CEO of Life Success Strategies Inc., is a professional speaker, leadership trainer, management consultant, life coach and inspirational author. Marc's background as a successful technology executive in the Silicon Valley, as an entrepreneur in California and Hawaii and with more than a decade studying peak performance and personal development allows him to bring a unique approach to supporting a new generation of leaders in claiming their power, achieving their dreams and tapping into their inner wisdom.

People who get what they want
are committed to it and clear about it.
– Marc Carignan

Marc is a student of many master teachers including Anthony Robbins, James Ray, Robert Kiyosaki, John Demartini, and others. He has achieved successes in all areas of his life and now focuses on teaching others how to make rapid and dramatic changes in their own lives. Marc supports people in living the lives they truly desire, personally and professionally, through speaking, training, coaching and authoring various educational materials including books and CDs, available for self-study. Marc is a Certified Life Coach and credentialed by the International Coach Federation.

To contact Marc or to learn more about products and services available, visit Life Success Strategies on the web at www.LifeSuccessStrategies.com, or call the United States offices of Life Success Strategies at 1-619-299-1700.

Acknowledgments

I am thankful and grateful for the assistance and support I've received leading up to, and during, the creation of this book. I thank my family-of-origin, for their constant belief in me and my work in the world: my parents Maurice and Denise; my brother Paul and his wife Heather, and children Jason and Vanessa; and my sister Nicole and her husband David. Coming from a close French Canadian family, I also thank "ma tante" Jeannine, and my cousins Chris and Dave and their families. I am where I am in my life today in large part due to the love and support of this extended family who saw a greater vision for me during the times when my outlook was not so clear.

Thanks also go to Peter Reding and Marcia Collins for their inspired contribution to the world, with respect to Coach For Life (coachforlife.com), from which I earned my coaching certification, and for creating the Foundation for Inspired Learning (inspiredlearning.org), a source of powerful and inspirational accelerated learning technologies. I thank them both for allowing me to include some magnificent information about the foundation and how it's changing the lives of so many people throughout the world.

Love and gratitude go to my life coach, Kendal Texeira, for her constant support of my work and my mission in life. Thanks to my business coach, James Malinchak, for his practical marketing and business savvy. Thank you to Marijo and Lee Franklin, my previous executive coaches, who each individually inspired within me tremendous personal and professional growth and a desire to intentionally follow my own path, leading me to pursue this work and to share my learnings and passion with others. Love and appreciation also go to an early reviewer of this book, Ellen Wright-Montgomery; thanks for your friendship, your assistance in creating this book and the difference you are making in the lives of so many young college-bound students in the state of California. You are a true social visionary.

For all who have touched and supported me, having been part of my story to this point in my life, I thank you and wish you joy, love and peace always. Namaste!

LEADERSHIP

INTENTION

VISION

PRACTICE

CONFIDENCE

ATTITUDE

LEARNING

Chapter 1. Leadership Starts on the Inside

The Journey of Personal Leadership

You can't take someone else to a place that you haven't been. Leaders must go there first.
– Anthony Robbins

Leading by Intention is a Choice

We are all leaders. Some of us simply don't know it yet.

Each one of us has the capacity to lead yet few of us ever truly claim this power. Many of us live in a world where our feelings, our choices and our realities are dictated by what's going on around us. This tends to create more of the same. Yes, people can work up the "corporate ladder" and other ladders of advancement in our societies but it tends to be a stepwise movement. There is another way.

The practice of creating your life deliberately requires intention. Leading by intention is taking responsibility for your life, accountability for your results, and having a clear vision of what you desire. The leaders who lead by intention in the world are few, yet those who live by this model are powerful creators. They tend to experience greater leaps of growth and success. They set larger goals and take greater risks. They enroll others to join in and participate in creating their desires.

Such "intentional leaders" create powerful visions for the future. They become clear about what they intend to create and align themselves "within" in order to focus their energy on creating those results. With this powerful internal alignment comes inner strength, influence upon others wanting and willing to participate in the goal, and abundance in every area of life. Leadership by intention is the practice of creating the life you desire, moment to moment, with ease, power and passion. This is *Leading from the Inside Out.*

Moving Past Fear

Ask yourself, "Am I living the life I desire?" Most of us have people or situations in our lives that please us, that we are really happy about. Most of us also have parts of our lives that we would prefer to be different, such as choices that we may see presented to us at work and in life, or the people we would like to attract into our lives, or our current financial or physical conditions. If we are all leaders within, why don't we have what we truly want in all areas? Wasn't life meant to be abundant?

Why do so many people settle for where they are? In my experience, fear is the primary reason. Fear is the reason that people don't achieve what they truly desire, whether it's due to fear of failure, rejection, embarrassment, or even the fear of success itself. Over time, fear compounds and affects their self-esteem, making the possibility of living the life they desire less likely and encouraging them to lower their expectations and "settle" for the way things are.

The solution to creating the life you desire in all areas is in releasing fear by moving into trust and faith. There is a continuum in life from fear to faith. Where you choose to live your life on this continuum is your choice. Let me explain.

Fear is an alert system that all animals possess, including humans. Fear is a stimulus to action, preparing animals for a fight or flight response. Our fear mechanism served us well in the early days of human evolution, running from a tiger or getting out of the way of a charging elephant. Those days are all but over now.

As humans we have a rational mind to help us make sense of these alerts and the world around us, giving us the ability to make more intelligent decisions than other animals. Our minds allow us to analyze situations and, with the power of abstract thinking, allow us to devise intelligent plans of action. With the power of our will, we can then take action. Taking action allows us to address the underlying problem causing the fear and to reduce or eliminate our feelings of fear. A part of this is releasing the physical manifestations of fear in our bodies.

There is a simple process to move through fear, one that starts with first noticing our fear response. Once we have received this signal, we can use the power of our minds to change it into faith. Before we discuss the process in detail, let us first better define faith.

Faith and Trust

The faith I speak of isn't religious faith, although it is compatible with religious principles. This faith means to trust deeply. It is trusting that there are Universal Laws in our world that have been observed, described and documented through thousands of years of human civilization. For example, a law that we are all familiar with is the Law of Gravity. We have learned that this is a law because it works consistently, whether we know exactly how it operates or not. It operates regardless of our actions, inactions, likes or dislikes. Certainly there are other laws and actions that may influence this law, but the fact remains that gravity works the same way, each and every time.

Universal Laws operate in a similar way. Each law works in the same way, each and every time. Just as ignorance of the Law of Gravity does not protect us from falling off a cliff if we step too close to the edge, ignorance of Universal Laws does not prevent us from feeling their effects. Before we continue discussing Universal Laws, let us step back and present a simple process for turning fear into faith.

Turning Fear into Faith

By turning your fears into faith, you allow yourself to move forward and take actions, risks and steps necessary to address the underlying problem and then shift your attention to achieving your desires. Try the process described by the following steps, as described in the book, "Rays of the Dawn," by Dr. Thurman Fleet. (This book is the basis for a body-mind-soul practice called Concept Therapy; visit the website concept-therapy.org for more information.)

1. Start by using your rational mind to determine the cause of the fear. Ask yourself, "What is the fear alerting you to? What potential danger are you being warned about?" Honor your fear mechanism by interpreting the signs.

2. Next, use the power of your rational mind to create a plan of action, taking some "intelligent action" immediately. By intelligent action, I

mean action that will address, or begin to address, the source of the fear identified above. This could be making a phone call, writing a letter, or taking some other step to resolve the problem. Because of the way humans are wired, if you do not take some immediate action, you will internalize the physical effects of the fear response. When fear turns inward, it can cause you to experience potentially life-damaging consequences, including rapid heart rate, high blood pressure, gastro-intestinal problems, anxiety, and depression. Therefore, taking some positive action without delay is critical.

3. If it is not within your power to eliminate the fear, ask for help. Talk to someone who may be able to help with an expert opinion (such as a doctor, a lawyer, a therapist or a coach), a second point of view (from a friend, family member or trusted advisor) or simply with someone you trust to share your concerns. Then take some action based upon your discussion. If nothing can be done immediately, then at least go for a walk, exercise at the gym, or meditate for clarity and guidance. Often any positive action is better than no action. This type of "alternate" positive action will help you in the short-term by alleviating the physical manifestations of the fear until you can take action that will address the underlying problem directly.

4. Finally, it is important that you do not fear anything needlessly. It has been said that there is more fear in the world than there is to be afraid of. Don't give the fear more power that it requires. Taking immediate action will normally alleviate the fear, giving you the opportunity to take further actions to resolve the fear without feeling the often intense physical manifestations of fear in your body. If you still feel fear, repeat this process handling each part of the fear using your rational mind to determine an intelligent solution to each part and then to take action. Once the cause of the fear is handled, you can then fully release the fear knowing that you have handled it and the underlying problem has been resolved to the best of your ability. Ultimately, that is all you can be expected to do.

Get moving. You can't correct
your course standing still.
– Marc Carignan

This process is designed to work with the normal human mental and physical responses that accompany fear. It allows emotional and intellectual resolution of underlying problems that are uncovered in working the process. Try it the next time you feel fear coming on and watch as you begin to move through the steps to arrive at a place of greater comfort, calm and resolution. Next, let's review the Universal Laws previously mentioned.

Universal Laws

The Laws

There are 7 primary laws, referred to as the Universal Laws. From a religious perspective, we can say that the Universal Laws describe, in part, the natural laws that God put into place in our Universe. From a scientific perspective, we can say that the Universal Laws describe how Energy moves and flows in our Universe.

The Universal Laws are:

1. Law of Perpetual Transmutation of Energy.
2. Law of Relativity.
3. Law of Vibration – and Attraction.
4. Law of Polarity.
5. Law of Rhythm.
6. Law of Cause and Effect.
7. Law of Gender – and Gestation.

Although these laws sometimes have name variations, they are the same laws. These laws define the order of our Universe, the truths of our existence in the physical world.

Law of Perpetual Transmutation of Energy

First is the Law of Perpetual Transmutation of Energy. This law says that everything is energy. The science of Albert Einstein and other brilliant quantum physicists and scientists have demonstrated in recent years the validity of this principle. They have proven that energy is in a constant state of motion. It is always vibrating. It is continually moving from one place to another, as electricity does while traveling in a copper wire.

Transmutation says that energy is always changing from one form to another. For example, a light bulb transmutes electrical energy into light and heat, causing it to glow and also to get warm to the touch. The energy of ocean waves is another example. The waves transmute the energy within its motion into sounds (the crashing of the waves), temperature changes near the shoreline (usually cooler by the shore) and the movement of the sands.

Law of Relativity

The second law is the Law of Relativity. It says that nothing is better or worse, bigger or smaller, heavier or lighter except in relation to something else. Without anything to compare to, everything "just is." This law may seem overly simplistic, but it describes a truth of our existence. We continually compare things in order to navigate our world.

There is power in realizing that our perceptions are simply points of view and not the truth. This awareness prevents us from falling into the trap of believing there is only one way to do something or that there are limited choices available to us. Knowledge of this law gives us more choices, greater flexibility and real power as leaders in the world.

Law of Vibration – and Attraction

The Law of Vibration is the third law. It states that since energy vibrates and that everything is energy, then everything vibrates. Nothing rests. The differences in energy are primarily the levels of vibration, known as the "frequency." This is also how radio waves work, allowing us to tune into a particular station by changing the radio dial (the reception frequency) to the station broadcasting what we want to hear.

An important sub-law is the Law of Attraction. This law is one of the most powerful and practical laws. It has been the subject of much discussion, interpretation and practical application over the centuries. It has also been the subject of recent movies and books including, "The Secret," "Ask and It Is Given," and "Pass It On," all on the suggested reading list (at the end of the book).

Who we are as human beings, from a religious perspective, has been described in every world tradition. Various religions and traditions refer to us as children of God, extensions of Source Energy or beings with the God-Presence within. From a scientific perspective, we are "energy." As energy, we are similar to and connected to all other forms of energy in the world. As our entire physical world is made of energy, we are therefore connected to all things including those that we would consider living and those that are not. As humans, our energy includes a consciousness and inner power. This consciousness and power allows us to transform energy, beginning with our thoughts, into the physical manifestations we desire.

Everything you desire starts first as a thought. With sufficient power and intention behind your thoughts, things materialize in your world. The Law of Attraction is the force behind this activity, bringing you into alignment with that which matches your energy vibration. Basically, the energy you put out in the world is what you get back. The Bible says that what you reap is what you sow. You must plant the seeds before the plant can grow. This is a fundamental truth of life as expressed by eastern and western traditions and now being proved by modern science.

Energy flows where attention goes.
– Various

Another way to look at Attraction is to realize that we focus on expands. As everything is energy, wherever attention goes, energy flows. Focusing on the negative brings more negative and focusing on the positive brings more positive. Choose where you place your attention wisely. (We will discuss the Law of Attraction in more detail in the next chapter.)

Law of Polarity

The Law of Polarity is the fourth law. This law says that everything has an opposite, such as hot and cold, good and bad, up and down. There is a positive and a negative, or one extreme to another, in everything. Again this is a perception as we interpret our world. We see something and compare it. We try to make sense of our world by measuring, weighing, comparing and analyzing. It is fundamental to how we operate. This law speaks of a continuum with "poles," like the north and south poles of our planet. Similar in nature to the Law of Relativity, this law does more than compare our experiences in relation to each other. This laws sets outer boundaries for our perceptions.

Law of Rhythm

The fifth law is the Law of Rhythm. Everything in our world has a rhythm or cycle. The tides move in and out, day follows night, the moon wanes and waxes, the earth has its seasons, and all living things experience a cycle of youth, middle age, old age and physical death. There are good times and bad times. There are rhythms throughout life.

As we become more attuned, we can see that there are natural rhythms all around us. With this knowledge, it becomes easier for us to accept when things are not going exactly as planned, sometimes due to various rhythms in life playing out. Just as you wouldn't want to try and surf against the tide, you must learn to work with these natural cycles in order to become an effective creator in the world.

Law of Cause and Effect

The Law of Cause and Effect is the sixth law. Every cause has an effect and every effect has its cause. All mechanical devices, including planes, trains and automobiles, all operate because of this law. Propulsion of automobiles is a great example. For autos to move, they must exert pressure by turning the wheels. This is done with cranks, belts and other systems, driven by pistons, cams and even more mechanical devices. Eventually, enough force is created to "push off" and send the car forward. Without cause and effect, usually initiated by a human driver, the car would never move at all.

Law of Gender – and Gestation

Finally, the seventh law is the Law of Gender. This law says that male and female are required for procreation, that there are masculine and feminine energies. As humans, male and female, we all have both so-called masculine and feminine energies within us. Chinese philosophy, for example, speaks of the yin (for the feminine) and yang (for the masculine) existing within all of nature, including humans.

This law also states that there is a gestation period for everything. Nothing happens instantaneously. There is always a waiting period, an amount of time that must pass for something to materialize or to mature. Whether it's a nine-month gestation period for a human child to progress from conception to birth or the time required for plantings of tulip bulbs in autumn to bloom in the spring, everything requires time.

Trying to rush gestation is usually not possible. Occasionally, unique growing conditions can cause a faster development period, but in general the differences are not significant. Fertile soil may cause faster blooms, hardier plants, and larger fruit. However, there is still a waiting period for the plant to germinate, grow, become strong, photosynthesize, and bloom. Only then can it bear fruit.

The Most Powerful Truths

I find that the most powerful truths are those that are often the simplest and most elegant. There is this sense of "ah-ha" when one hears or reads a Universal Law, a sense of having known that before, having learned it elsewhere or even having experienced it in their own lives. Now that you know these laws, you have the opportunity to more consciously direct your intention and power in alignment with these laws, creating your desired life more easily, surfing "with" the waves of life.

Tapping Into Your Inner Leader

There are two ways of exerting one's strength;
one is pushing down, the other is pulling up.
– Booker T. Washington, born into slavery;
became an American educator, author and
early 20th century leader of the African
American community

Your Code of Honor

True leadership starts from within. You must be a leader in your own life before becoming a truly effective leader of others. There are several aspects of personal leadership, being a leader in one's own life. A key strategy to effective personal leadership is adopting a Code of Honor.

In the times of courageous warriors, there were Codes of Honor. These codes defined not simply rules to follow, but practices that warriors would adhere to and consequences if they did not. Such codes were put in place to create trust among the warriors and in so doing better protect the army from outside attack. It created a sense of community, identity and brotherhood among the warriors. In this military setting, there were also serious consequences if these codes were broken.

In our modern world, we typically are not risking our physical well-being on a daily basis, as was true in the age of ancient warriors. A Code of Honor, however, is still a powerful tool that can be used by those desiring to create an intentional life. It's a tool for use by leaders choosing to author their own lives and create their own destinies.

Codes of Honor speak of respect, commitment, integrity, accountability and responsibility. They describe how members of a group stand for certain principles, commit to adhering to certain policies, and affirm a sense of trust and loyalty. They also set expectations for individuals within the group.

All great people have had Codes of Honor, ethical agreements with themselves and their world. These codes are expressed through words and actions. They separate greatness from mediocrity.

Following are ideas for creating a personal Code of Honor. Start with your own standards. Then, if you choose, you can extend these principles beyond yourself to your family, community, workplace and associations of all kinds.

One note: Many Codes of Honor of the past speak in terms of negatives, such as "Never disparage yourself or minimize your strength or power." I prefer and recommend stating your Codes of Honor in the positive, honoring the Law of Attraction, by focusing on what you want to create rather than what you want to avoid. In this example, you might change this statement to read "I respect myself under all circumstances, regardless of my results." You might also add "I remember that I am strong, powerful and resilient."

A Personal Code of Honor

- I respect myself under all circumstances, regardless of the outcome.
- I remember that I am strong and powerful.
- I courageously face the truth in every area of my life.
- I take 100% responsibility for my life, taking full accountability of any consequences.
- I demonstrate respect for myself when I respect others.
- I am slow to anger and quick to forgive.

How would your life be different if you created and adhered to your own personal Code of Honor? How would your life be different if you really acknowledged the power you have within you and "unleashed" it in your world?

How you treat yourself is an indication to others about how you should be treated. This is a key point as all your personal and professional relationships draw from your relationship with yourself, your place of self-honoring and self-respect. To what extent do you honor and respect yourself, not from an egocentric perspective but from a truly empowering one? Choose to be your own best supporter, the person who most believes in "you!"

The Road to Mastery

Success is a lousy teacher. It seduces smart
people into thinking they can't lose.
– Bill Gates

Results Are Feedback

How many people do you know that measure their value as a person, as a leader, as an employee or as a parent by their results? Have you ever heard someone saying to themselves that they must be a bad parent because of what their children do or a bad employee because they can't seem to please their boss? This is not a leader's perspective.

Leaders who lead by intention know that results are not a measure of self-worth. They realize that results are powerful feedback on the effects of their actions. They realize that the Law of Cause and Effect is always at work, that when they take an action (a cause) it will always create some effect. These leaders then use their results as a way to "fine tune" their actions, thereby changing their results.

"Who" you are, as a person, as a leader, and as a creator in the world, is independent of your results. That is, your inherent value is not based on what you do but on who you are. Yet, in our modern world, we are often judged by what we accomplish, who we beat in the marketplace or on the golf course, or how much money we make.

The Softball Game

Here's an example. Say you are a member of a neighborhood softball team. You have practiced with your team every weekend. You have good rapport with the members of your team. You each know the position you play and have learned each other's strengths on the field. You are now ready to play against another team, a visiting team.

At the end of the first inning, you look at the scoreboard and it reads "Visitors 0, Home 1." Your team scored a run. Let's say that it's now the end of the eighth inning and the scoreboard now reads "Visitors 3. Home 2." What happened? Since your team, the home team, is down by one run what might you do to try to win?

You might consider various strategies. One strategy that many people seem to do in the real world is to "play the scoreboard." That is, they would simply go to the scoreboard and change the score, perhaps to "Visitors 3. Home 4," by changing the home score from 2 to 4. Is that the way to play the game? Of course not. Haven't you seen this show up in the real world though?

You see, people often choose to simply ignore the scoreboard in their life, or they say to their friends that the umpire is crooked, or the game is fixed, or that the team must be tired today. My favorite is the statement, "It's only a game." Well, of course it's only a game, but didn't you "intend" to win?

These behaviors in playing games are similar to ignoring reality, or ignoring current results, or making excuses about results that did occur in real life. Many people often just want to feel better about their life or about what's going on and don't look at what's really happening. They may somehow redefine what's really happening to soothe themselves from feeling the pain of the truth. People often lie to themselves. Or they ignore the facts. Others downplay the importance of their results.

How You Play the Game

What I've learned in my years in management, leadership and coaching is that how people play games is how they "play their life." People who cheat in games tend to cheat in life. If they are good-natured when playing games, they are typically good-natured in life. How people think, talk and act when things are going well is easy. People tend to "look good" when everything's going their way. This is when people are the most calm and collected. This is when everything's going according to plan.

You know that things don't always turn out exactly as you've planned. There are often exceptions. There are always twists and turns. The real test is how you react when things do not go as planned, when things are not going exactly as you'd hoped. Do you resist or downplay results you don't like? Do you get angry or frustrated? Do you resign yourself in disappointment or depression? Do you blame someone else, or some external factor like the weather, the economy, or some other event?

What if things are going better than expected? Are you grateful and respectful? Are you arrogant and boastful? Do you imagine yourself to be infallible and hence take unwarranted risks? These are all indicative of how you engage in life.

Getting back to the softball game, we all know that there are rules that you agree to when you decide to play. These rules "level the playing field," creating a set of expectations defining how you and others agree to play and what it takes to win or lose the game. In fact, every game has an agreed upon set of rules and a definition of how you win. In order for you to master any game, you must first understand the rules.

The rules of softball, as in the rules of all sports, do not allow players to change the scores on the scoreboard itself when they don't like the results. This isn't the point of the scoreboard. After all, the game is not played "on the scoreboard." The game is played "on the field." The scoreboard is simply an accounting of the results that have occurred on the field. It is a "reflection" of reality.

Don't be mad at the scoreboard. It is an impartial measure of your results. What good is it to judge yourself or others harshly by the scoreboard? It is simply feedback. Yet it is important. It's a indication of what's working and what's not. It's telling you how well your strategy is working out, how well your actions are causing your intended results. Perhaps you need to reconsider your strategy. To change the score, you must change what's happening on the field! This goes for any game you might play.

This sounds really simple, and it is. Yet how often do you give up when things aren't going your way? How often do you tell yourself something that isn't really true just to feel better? Did you "intend" to win? (We will discuss intention in greater detail shortly.)

A Key to Mastery

A key to mastery is to see the scoreboard for what it truly is. It's not "who" you are, it's just telling you "where" you are. It's giving you feedback about what's happening on the playing field, regardless of whether you are playing a game of softball or playing the game of life. The only way to make any changes, or even to get any score at all on the scoreboard, is to get in the game. You have to get on the field and play. If you need to take a "time out" to rest and strategize, do so. But then, get back in the game.

The point of any game is to play to win, not to avoid losing. Avoiding losing the game is not the same as intending to win it. The easiest way to avoid losing is simply not to play. To have an opportunity to win, you must play. You must intend to win. You must look at your results along the way. You must see if you are on track, or if your results are not as you expected.

Intentional leaders use results as feedback to make adjustments in their actions. They don't use the scores to judge themselves harshly. To change your results, change your actions. To change your actions, you must remain on the playing field. The people in the stands watching the game are not playing the game, even if they are shouting and screaming. They are only spectators.

Failure is the opportunity to
begin again, more intelligently.
– Henry Ford

In the game of life, undesired results often look like failures. They are not truly failures. You only fail if you choose to stop playing. Undesirable results are only feedback. We often learn more by making mistakes along the way since we learn how "not" to do something, that is we learn what actions do not create our intended results. This is very useful information. The more you play any game, the more mistakes you will make. However, the more you play, the more you also develop winning strategies that work. Let's look, then, at the scoreboards in the game of life.

Wealth in All Areas of Life

The Scoreboards of Life

Although more complex than softball, each area of your life has one or more scoreboards that give you feedback on how effectively you are playing the game of life. As a whole, these scores represent your current level of "wealth" in all areas of your life.

What are the scoreboards in your life? I look at life in five areas, or with five sets of scoreboards: financial, relational, intellectual, physical and spiritual. Taken together, you have a master scoreboard for your life. One of my teachers, James Ray, calls these five areas taken together, "Harmonic Wealth."

These scoreboards, just as in softball, do not reflect your intrinsic value as a person or as a player of the game, but rather they reflect how effectively you are playing and creating your intended results. Look at the results in your life plainly and honestly in order to make the adjustments necessary to be successful.

Financial Wealth

The first area is financial wealth. In this area, a typical scoreboard is the balance in your bank account. Just as a softball game isn't played on the scoreboard, neither is the money game. That is, the money game is not played at your bank. It's not played in your checkbook register either. It's played in your life. In life, this includes income from your businesses, jobs, investments, rental or royalty income, and various other "streams of income."

The point of mastery is in getting good at the game itself. Your bank account then becomes the scoreboard for how well you're doing at playing the game. This is a viewpoint that investment expert and billionaire Warren Buffett shares. He has publicly stated that although he doesn't need any more money, he sees his financial net worth and its growth as a convenient and effective measure of the success of his investment strategies. Buffett, one of the world's wealthiest men, knows that his net worth is simply a scoreboard for the money game. It indicates how well he's playing the game "on the field" of money.

Money was never a big motivation for me, except as a way to keep score. The real excitement is playing the game.
– Donald Trump

Allow me to repeat this point. Your bank account is not the scoreboard for who you are, or for how worthy you are. It is, however, an impartial and accurate indication of how well you've mastered the money game. Just as experienced softball players tend to get better and more consistent results on the field, the same is true in each of life's "games." In the money game, the more effective, experienced, educated and consistent you are, the higher your score – and the bigger your bank account!

Relational Wealth

The next area is relational wealth. What is your "love score?" Have you attracted and maintained wonderful loving relationships in your life? Remember, don't blame the scoreboard if you haven't. Likewise, there's no need to thank it either. It's just feedback. The game of love is played on the field of love, in the world of relationships.

Are you playing the game fully or are you on the sidelines? Perhaps you are simply in the stands cheering others on but not really playing. Are you afraid of losing the game, and just hanging out in the stands watching other people play? Take an honest look at your relationship scoreboards, and don't judge yourself too critically. Rather, honestly review where you are and use this information to make any course corrections you may choose in order to achieve your relational desires.

Specific scoreboards for married or partnered people may be the frequency of "date nights" with your spouse, the time you spend with your children, and the "fun index" of the time you all spend together. Single scoreboards could include the number of dates, or "first dates," with potential partners. Don't forget, whether married, partnered or single, your relationship with yourself is important as well. Determine what you choose to do to honor, respect and celebrate who you are in the world!

Intellectual Wealth

The third area is intellectual wealth. A scoreboard for employees is usually their position within the company. Are you moving up the corporate ladder? Are you up for a promotion? For entrepreneurs and business owners, the scoreboard could relate to the success of your marketing and sales efforts, the number of customers in your database, the quality of your products and services, the impact your company is making in your industry, association and business notoriety and accolades, and the growth of your company. For students, scoreboards include test grades, reports cards, and the progression in a field of study toward the attainment of an academic degree or certification.

Be a yardstick of quality.
Some people aren't used to an environment
where excellence is expected.
– Steve Jobs

Physical Wealth

Physical wealth has many scoreboards, the most infamous being the bathroom scale. How many times have people screamed at this scoreboard! It's not happy for you when you drop those extra pounds or angry with you after getting back from an all-you-can-eat cruise. The scale is just telling you the score: your weight. I'm not here to debate the value of this particular scoreboard in the health and fitness game, but it is a scoreboard that has its place.

Another scoreboard might be a wellness score, such as how often you are healthy in a given year. Other scoreboards include body fat percentages, your ability to run a marathon within a certain time, or the maturing of your body into a healthy old age. Pick the scoreboards that you want to follow but don't get mad at the scoreboards. Don't ignore them either. Each one provides a piece of the puzzle, a part of the overall score that measures your physical well-being.

Spiritual Wealth

Finally, we move to the spiritual wealth scoreboards. These are perhaps the most personal scoreboards of all. It may be to think about how often you experience "peace of mind," moments where you are centered, calm and connected. For religious people, this would include adherence to the tenets and principles of your religious tradition. How often do you feel connected to something greater than your physical body? Think about how often you put yourself in situations where you're feeling "in touch" with the magnificence of creation, such as walking in nature, reaching out to help others as a volunteer or simply helping out a friend or neighbor.

Are there specific people, places and things that inspire you to take positive actions in your life? Have you developed a powerful sense of intuition? Have you learned to trust your hunches and the "gut feelings" that you have? Are you feeling calm and joyful about life, whether or not you like the scores you're seeing, knowing that you have the power to influence the scores? Are you on a path of growing consciousness and enlightenment? Choose the scoreboards that resonate with you!

Review Your Scoreboards

What are your specific scoreboards? What scores give you the feedback to know if you're "on track" with where "you" want to go and with what you want to achieve in your life. There are no right and wrong scoreboards. Decide what you want then determine the best ways to honestly measure how you're doing. Many people don't really know what they want. This creates a problem in measurement. When you know what you truly want, ideas and methods to attain them begin appearing in your life.

Whatever you do, keep playing the game. The point of life is to play the game: to learn, to love and to grow. Haven't you heard the expression, "It isn't whether you win or lose, it's how you play the game." The core truth is that how you play the game, including your attitude, your confidence, your clarity, your code of honor and more, shows up in everything you do and is the real joy of playing. Winning or losing isn't the point either, but it does provide feedback on how you are playing.

In the deliberate playing of any game, you become more masterful. As you learn more about the rules and the strategies of the game, you become more masterful. As you learn from those that are already masters in the game, you also become more masterful. The same is true of the games of life. And like all games, they are supposed to be fun and joyful, causing us to grow and stretch. The best and most powerful games in life give us opportunities to more fully claim our greatness and experience the joy of living fully.

Don't get me wrong. Make winning the game your goal. The point, however, is to fully play the game. With sufficient practice, knowledge and experience, you can win any game you play including the money game. It is in playing a game fully that one achieves the greatest rewards in life.

Service is a Privilege of Leadership

The best way to find yourself is to lose yourself in the service of others.
– Mohandas "Mahatma" Gandhi

Contributing Beyond Yourself

Service is one of the greatest callings, or privileges, of any true leader. Mostly we have spoken of claiming your own leadership power from within. This is an important first step, but there's more available. When you step into leadership beyond yourself and your own personal needs, you move into a special and honorable place of service to others. Because of the Law of Attraction, the more you give, the more the Universe returns to you. In helping others, you help yourself.

Perhaps the most powerful rallying call of any leader comes from the question, "How can I serve?" In what ways can you serve others? In what ways would you like to serve? And how might you serve the Greater Good? For religious people, in what ways do you choose to serve God?

What Is Your Purpose?

As an intentional leader, you must have a purpose. This purpose can be one you choose, such as eradicating hunger in your community or helping disadvantaged children. It may be to serve as a wonderful role model for your children and your community. It may be to write a book to serve people who you may never meet, but are called to support.

Rather than choose their purpose consciously, some people get clear about their purpose by listening to an inner voice or a God-inspired calling. Your purpose can come to you in many different ways. In fact, you may already know your purpose. Or you may be searching for it. Maybe you've never really thought of yourself on this larger scale, believing that you could make a difference in the world. When you tap into the power of intentional leadership, anything is possible. When you truly connect with your purpose, it undoubtedly will have an element of service. As you address your own needs, you create greater opportunities to care for and serve others.

Never doubt that a small group of thoughtful,
committed citizens can change the world.
Indeed, it is the only thing that ever has.
– Margaret Mead, a mid-20th century
American cultural anthropologist

The Story of Ryan's Well

At the age of 6, a young boy named Ryan Hreljac (pronounced, HERL-jack) learned that many people in Africa did not have access to safe, clean drinking water. Without access to clean water, he learned that people were dying every day, including many children. He set out to raise $70 to build a well in Africa to help a village gain access to clean water. By performing extra chores around the house and asking friends and neighbors for donations, young Ryan achieved this goal in just four months.

Unfortunately, the information he had received was inaccurate. The cost for building a well in Africa was actually quite a bit more. In fact, the cost was $2,000. Undeterred, he continued on his mission to raise the remaining money to achieve his goal of building a well in Africa. By this time, many people in his small Canadian town had learned of his quest and wrote articles about him and his project in local papers. Other children in his school also became excited about his project and volunteered to work with Ryan to help him achieve the larger financial goal. Ryan was even interviewed on local radio and TV stations. As you can imagine, it did not take long for him to earn the remaining money.

Upon achieving his goal, Ryan (and his mother) met with a local representative of a non-profit organization in Canada focused on African clean water projects. It was decided with Ryan's guidance that his well would be built near a school. A school in Uganda, where children from several nearby villages attended, was selected. His well was built and was dedicated a year later. The school and community leaders named it, "Ryan's Well."

To dedicate his well in person, Ryan was invited to visit Africa as a guest of the local people who had benefitted from his gift. They wanted to meet this child who had done what so many adults could not do. Ryan had successfully inspired and led a project to bring safe, clean water to a needy community in Africa. Hundreds of children and families welcomed Ryan (again, with his mother) to dedicate his life-giving well. The village was so inspired by his visit and his gift that the school wrote and sang a song for Ryan.

While still in Africa, Ryan was further inspired. Before he left he was already learning about what would be required to provide clean water for other schools and villages. He learned about portable drilling equipment. He also learned about other areas with children that needed clean water most urgently.

In the 10 years since, Ryan Hreljac has raised over $1.5 million dollars through the Ryan's Well Foundation, which has continued to sponsor clean water projects throughout the most needy parts of Africa. Still a young man at the age of 16, he was inspired to act and he followed through. In so doing, he inspired others to join with him, a sign of a powerful, intentional leader.

Ryan's inspiration has touched millions of people. If a 6-year-old boy can start such a movement, what could you do? Ryan Hreljac has appeared on The Oprah Winfrey Show twice, has spoken with countless children in schools throughout the United States and Canada, and is a much sought-after motivational speaker. He continues to make a difference by his vision, his commitment, and by being in service to a cause greater than himself. In fact, he created the Ryan's Well Foundation, and the corresponding Canadian website ryanswell.ca, to educate people and raise funds for additional water projects. According to this source, his one original well in Uganda has now grown to 266 wells in 12 countries, serving an estimated 435,343 people.

Become Inspired

Inspiration can come from anywhere. We all know it when we feel it, because although it normally shows up in our mind as "inspired thought," it comes with a powerful "gut feeling" or a sense of intuition. Many of us are inspired by reading stories of great men and women and how they overcame their challenges. Others are inspired by playing competitive sports and some by listening to a beautiful piece of music or by appreciating a wonderful piece of art. A favorite way for me to be inspired is to walk in nature, especially climbing mountain trails, enjoying the flora and fauna along the way.

Ultimately what inspiration does is tap into the power within. It brings a sense of alignment with the truth of who we really are and what we are capable of in the world. It also encourages us to take action. When you do receive inspired thought, it is often wise to take the "inspired action" suggested. Intentional leaders honor both their rational minds and their intuitive sense. (We'll discuss action further in a later chapter.)

The best way to be and stay inspired is to do what you love. If you love to play music, do that. If you love teaching people, do that. If you love fixing cars, then do that. When you do what you love, you live your life with passion. You connect to your heart. Great service always comes from the heart. Coming from this place, you also inspire others to find their passions, indirectly serving others as well. In fact, you cannot prevent yourself from helping others when you are living your passions because you become a model and an inspiration for other people.

The road to your dreams is not often a busy road. Few people stay committed to their dreams and consistently move in the direction of their desires. The numbers of footprints in the path in front of you get fewer as you go along. Sometimes people fear that you are changing by following your dreams. Some may even confront you, claiming that you're foolish or that you aren't likely to succeed. By succeeding, you may make some people uncomfortable. When these challenging moments occur, remember this: "Mediocrity always attacks excellence." Follow your dreams and passions and you'll create the life that most people only dream about. You may even inspire others to do the same!

LEADERSHIP

INTENTION

VISION

PRACTICE

CONFIDENCE

ATTITUDE

LEARNING

Chapter 2. Intention and Desire Are Powerful Magnets

Your Intentions Define Your Life

A good intention clothes itself with power.
– Ralph Waldo Emerson

Declaring Your Intentions

The power of intention is about choosing something that you want to achieve or create in your life, without needing to know how to accomplish it. It is treating something that may seem to be "impossible" and transforming it from a possibility to a reality. This is the process of manifesting in the physical world, where your thoughts and desires are transformed into reality. We called this step "declaring your intention," as you are deliberately stating your desires.

When you declare your intentions, you boldly state your vision and your corresponding commitment to its outcome. When you have developed the skills required to create clear intentions in your life and then to consistently make them come true, you have achieved true power in the physical world. Leadership is the responsible exercise of that power, within your own life and in ways that impact the lives of others and the world at large.

As you exercise your "intention muscle," you gain mastery. With mastery comes speed, shortening the time required to go from possibility to reality. This is the purpose of gaining mastery of intentional living: to create your intended results quickly and easily.

What Are Your Intentions?

What do you want? What do you intend to accomplish or attain? Toward what goal are you directing your mind? What purpose do you have for your life or for your work?

Intention speaks of the power of your mind. It is about directing your mind consciously. As your mind is always focused on something, you begin to gain power by first being aware of what you are tending to focus on in your life. Most of what you focus upon is unconscious, as the unconscious mind is working every minute of every day, whether you are awake or asleep. People exercise regular patterns of thought, usually without consciously thinking about what they're doing from moment to moment.

Have you noticed that much of what you do is on "automatic pilot?" Perhaps you drive the same route every time you go to work, to school, or to the gym? You probably start each day in pretty much the same way without thinking about it too much. Routines or habits can be very powerful, and we will be discussing these further in a later chapter.

For now, think about how much you do day to day just because it has become routine. An important step in mastering the power of intention is to increase your awareness of what you are thinking. What you focus upon and how you feel are the primary indications of what you are thinking about. You don't need to scan every thought to know what you are thinking. Simply reflect on what you tend to focus on, and how you feel about it.

For example, do you typically focus on what's missing in your life or are you noticing all that you already have? Do you feel like you are missing out on something or are you grateful and peaceful with the way your life is unfolding? Of course, there's also lots of middle ground between the pain and joy that these questions imply as well. The point isn't to judge yourself harshly but rather to become more attuned and aware of what you are focused upon.

Intentional Leaders

A true leader of intention is aware of what they focus on and what emotions they are experiencing. You see, everyone is always creating. We create our results everyday by our thoughts, our focus and our feelings. We can create a sense of well-being or we can create a state of frustration. We can welcome people we meet into our world or we can exclude them. We can joyously take on new work or we can resist it. In all our thoughts and all our choices, conscious or unconscious, we create.

When you become aware you begin to discover what your thoughts are primarily focused upon and therefore why you have created your current results, good and bad. In order to become more aware, it is important to tune into your self-talk. What are you telling yourself everyday? Are you your own best friend, encouraging yourself when you make mistakes or things don't go exactly as planned? Are you unreasonable or tough on yourself, beating yourself up with private messages of self-abuse? Perhaps you respect and even honor yourself publicly? I'm not speaking of unnecessary ego or conceit, but rather a healthy self-respect. Does this self-respect carry over into your private thoughts or just in your public persona? For example, would you ever tell your best friend things you tell yourself regularly in your "self-talk?"

The mind is everything.
What you think you become.
– Buddha

Everything that was ever created started out as just a thought. Put simply, thoughts create. Thoughts are pure potential energy. They either empower us or weaken us. When you hear encouraging words, are you empowered or weakened? When someone is critical or judgmental of you, how do you feel? Empowered or weakened? Wouldn't it follow that if you are telling yourself positive or negative things that your emotional state would reflect the intention of those words?

Specifically, intention is deliberate, directed thought. It is focused and clear. It defines the vision of what you what to create. It is taking something that you may have no idea of how to create and saying, "I don't know how, but I intend to find a way."

Living intentionally requires taking risks. It is also about respecting your own desires. In short, it describes what it is that you truly want to create. More than wanting, in fact, intention describes what you are committed to create.

If you want to see some high-energy "intentioners", look no further than young children. Children are intention-manifestation masters. When they really want something, there's no mistaking it. They'll ask for it, they'll jump up and down, and hang on to the idea day and night. They can really be persistent. Often children will drive adults a little crazy expressing their desires because they are so focused upon and unrelentless in what they want. Assuming they stay focused and don't give up, kids regularly manifest many of the things they really want. Are you as committed as an enthusiastic child to get what you want?

How Will You Do It?

Most people don't allow themselves to want what they truly want because they can't see how they're going to get it! So people often just "dream." Sure, dreaming is fine. But is it just a dream, or is it truly a desire that you want to manifest in the world? If you knew you could create anything you wanted, and that ultimately you could not fail in your attempts, what would you choose to create? What dreams and desires have you pushed deep down inside as foolish, or impossible? Are you willing to reconsider?

Before you do, let's talk more about how you will create your desired outcomes and the truth about it. There's a game I've often played to help demonstrate this point. Adults and kids alike love this game. The kid inside you will probably like it too!

The Intention-Mechanism Game

Imagine a room full of people with your friends, your family, or whomever else you'd like to imagine. Let's say you've assembled 100 people to play this game. I call this game the "Intention-Mechanism Game". To succeed at the game, each person, one at a time, must travel from one side of the room to the other. The rules are simple.

Each person must cross the room in a unique way, differently than anyone who has crossed before them. Each person must use a different method, or "mechanism," to cross the room. The other 99 people are the judges. If anyone notices someone repeat a mechanism in crossing the room, they must give the person crossing the verbal buzzer sound, "bzzzzzzz", and then that person must go back to the starting point and try again a different way, with a new mechanism. The game ends when everyone crosses successfully.

Let's start. At first, everyone is on one side of the room waiting to cross. People may form a line, or simply decide among themselves when they're up. As you can probably imagine, the earlier in the game that you cross the room, the easier it is. In a context of fun and learning, let's watch the first person cross.

Take the first step in faith. You don't have to
see the whole staircase. Just take the first step.
– Martin Luther King, Jr.

The first person simply walks across the room to the other side. It's the first successful crossing; the crowd cheers. Person # 2: This person gets down on the ground and crawls. It's another success. More cheers. The game continues this way, with each person crossing using a different mechanism. It's pretty easy until around person # 50, when the remaining 50 people waiting to cross are noticing that most of the mechanisms they were thinking of using have been tried. Those waiting to cross must pay careful attention to the people crossing ahead of them in order to avoid re-using a mechanism. As person # 50 crosses doing the "bunny hop," person # 51 starts sweating a little; that was her idea too. There's only a few seconds left now for person # 50 to finish hopping across the room, and for person # 51 to think of a new way to cross while waiting for her turn at the starting line. Good thing for gymnastics as a child, because at the last minute, person # 51 decides to "cartwheel" across the room. Everyone cheers for the exciting mechanism she used!

Now fast forward to person # 80. There have been 79 previous crossers, and now he must try to find something new. He hopes that no one has used his idea, since it's getting harder to remember what's been tried and what hasn't been. So, he does the "Rocky move," boxing his way across the room; he must have forgotten that person # 34 did that too, so he gets buzzed. People laugh, all in good fun. Person # 80 moves back to the starting point while thinking again of a new mechanism and then tries again. Within seconds, he's trying something new, this time doing the "bunny hop". Bzzzzzzz. Try again. Finally, he tries skipping across the room; he makes it this time, as he's apparently the first to skip across the room.

Not all of us can get 'there' the first time we try.
– Bill Bartmann, "The Billionaire Nobody Knows", as named by the Wall Street Journal

At last, person # 100 begins to cross, doing a "John Travolta disco dance" across the room and the game is won! Everybody wins! Everyone crossed successfully! One hundred unique mechanisms were used to cross the room! The crowd cheers and screams with joy. They all made it to the other side. They all made it, in fact, without knowing for sure how they would need to cross to win the game.

Debriefing the Game

Let's take a closer look at this game. Did you get the sense that people preparing to cross were delaying their choice of mechanism until the person just before them crossed? Each person probably had a few ideas in mind, but as more and more people crossed the room, their ideas were being used up right before their eyes. The people waiting to cross needed to stay focused on the people crossing ahead of them so they wouldn't miss what had been tried in order to avoid getting buzzed by repeating a mechanism.

Note that those people who got buzzed didn't lose the game. According to the rules of the game they simply had the opportunity to try again. Some people may have been buzzed more than once but with the intention of getting across each person found a way. Each came up with a mechanism that eventually worked. Some people who were waiting to cross may have also helped those who couldn't think of a way across, sharing some of their ideas. (Remember the rules of the game did not disallow anyone from helping fellow team members.)

This brings us to the key question regarding this game, the Intention-Mechanism Game. What percentage of the group's success do you believe came from intention (to cross the room according to the rules of the game) and what percentage came from the mechanism (the specific methods selected and used to cross the room)? Do you think that it was 50%-50%? Or was it perhaps 20% intention and 80% mechanism? Or even 80% intention and 20% mechanism?

Failure is the opportunity to begin again,
more intelligently.
– Henry Ford

I would like you to consider that the intention, or the "true resolve", was to cross the room no matter what! Each person had a clear intention to cross successfully, even if they didn't know exactly the strategy they would use to cross. They knew they would figure it out even if they didn't succeed on their first try. Perhaps they realized that they could ask for help if they needed it. Perhaps the task seemed simple enough and familiar enough that each person could cross successfully. Maybe some people believed that someone else would step up to help them if they needed it, perhaps if they asked for help? In any event, everyone was committed to cross no matter what – even if they were a little nervous about how they would do it. For those who didn't truly believe it, their team members held that belief on their behalf. The team's belief "trumped" any doubter's disbelief.

I propose that the ratio really is "Intention 100% - Mechanism 0%". What, 100%-0%? Yes! There was an overriding, clear intention by the team and each person on it. Of course there were various mechanisms used, one hundred of them to be exact. The mechanisms, however, were never the issue. They were simply how the game was played. They had nothing to do with the desire and intention to complete the game successfully, that is, to "win" the game. As you can see, there were probably an unlimited number of ways across. We could have played the game with 200, 300 or even 1,000 people and each person could have found a different way to cross. Although the mechanisms selected were the specific actions that took each person across, the choices were insignificant as long as they were different. It was really about being clear, being sure, and being committed to the intention of winning the game.

There are many paths to the top of the
mountain, but the view is always the same.
– Chinese proverb

This game demonstrates the true sense of intention: that the desired result of crossing the room was already a "sure thing" in each person's mind. Each person "expected" to cross the room successfully whether or not they did it the first time they tried. As a group, there was no doubt about the eventual success in the game, even if some people experienced various degrees of fear in getting ready to cross.

You see, there were many possible "paths" to the specific goal of winning the game. When you are this sure of something in your life, it must manifest. There is no other choice! What outcomes do you desire in your life? More importantly, what outcomes do you truly expect in your life?

Comparing Intentional and Traditional Leadership

Outlining the Leadership Styles

All great leaders, great inventors, and great visionaries did not know "how" they were going to create what they envisioned or intended in their lives, they just knew that they would find a way to make it come true. This is a different approach than that of traditional leadership. It has a different "context" for leadership.

In traditional leadership, whether in a personal or professional setting, the focus is typically on:

- predicting the future based on past evidence
- creating a vision and producing consensus to reach corresponding goals
- making feasible promises they can be counted on to keep
- reacting from past experiences, the way things have been done previously.

On the surface, these ideas seem quite reasonable, and much of the world operates in this way, day in and day out. Many things get done and move forward with this type of leadership. It is the way most leaders manage in the corporate world. It is also quite different from the concept of leading by intention, which is the mindset of many successful inventors, artists and entrepreneurs in the world.

When at their most powerful, intentional leaders share several attributes including:

- declaring the future without evidence
- creating context, taking a stand, and creating new possibilities
- making bold promises they don't know how to keep
- acting from the future, with the vision of the way it will be in the future clear in their minds.

Declaring the Future

Let's discuss each difference, or change in context, listed above. First, to declare the future based on no evidence means to step into the unknown. It is similar to having the intention to cross the room but not knowing how that might happen, knowing that you may have never crossed a room like the one you're going to cross today.

A great real world example of "declaring the future without evidence" is in the leadership of Nelson Mandela. His clear, unwavering intention of a free and united South Africa was very strong, yet to most people this seemed impossible at the beginning of his cause. After all, Mandela was living in the age of apartheid. He and a growing group of believers maintained a clear intention and kept shifting their mechanisms (such as in the methods people used to cross the room) with the goal of manifesting their intention. Their mechanisms ranged from civil disobedience and public violence in the early days to non-violence and global economic pressure in later years. Mandela's imprisonment fueled the country's resistance to unfair treatment and prompted those who were discriminated under apartheid to enroll the world in withdrawing their financial investments from the country. Many western countries complied, including the United States and much of Europe, until the powers of South Africa agreed to negotiate for a free and racially equal country.

There was no way for Mandela to know for sure how this goal would be reached. He undoubtedly had some ideas of what might transpire or what mechanisms would probably be required. As such, he changed his tactics many times along the way. Despite not knowing for sure, Mandela was clear of his goal. He was so clear that he began enrolling others in his vision of a free and united country! (We'll discuss vision more in a later chapter.)

Mandela persisted even after being imprisoned on Robben Island for 28 years. This prison, off the southern coast of South Africa near Cape Town, was an island prison much like the US prison that was Alcatraz in San Francisco Bay. He continued to advocate for a free and united South Africa upon his release. He kept his vision alive even while in prison, preparing himself for the day he would finally be released. His clear intention led the South African people, both blacks and whites, to create a new country, new opportunities for millions of South Africans, and new hope for millions of people in various forms of oppression throughout Africa. Mandela was shortly thereafter elected to his country's highest office, being the first black President of his country, overseeing the drafting and implementation of a new constitution. Although officially retired, he continues today to inspire millions of people in Africa and worldwide in supporting important African and global causes. Mandela's intention was 100% of his focus.

Notice how different this context was than the traditional leadership approach of predicting the future based on past evidence. How often have you or others around you made judgments about what was possible or not based on what you or they had previously done, or learned, or experienced. This is the way it is most often done, basing the future on how things have worked out in the past, or "how we've always done it." This is often used as a common defense for stating what is possible and what is not. Leading by intention breaks this mold and trusts a person's strength of intention in producing the results desired, rather than simply using past experiences to predict future results.

The future isn't what it used to be!
– Yogi Berra, former Major League Baseball player and manager, elected to the Baseball Hall of Fame

Creating Context

Now let's look at the ideas of "creating context, taking a stand, and creating new possibilities." This sounds very bold, and in many ways it is. It describes a very different approach than the traditional approach. Traditionally, people focus on "creating a vision and producing consensus to reach corresponding goals." Again, this seems very reasonable. Looking at the traditional approach, I would agree that vision is important, yet traditional visions tend to be primarily about content. Of course, content – that is, what you want to create – is important and necessary. This concept of vision, however, moves us a giant step forward in the intention model. The idea of a vision becomes a "context", an environment in which to "hold" the vision.

For example, it isn't sufficient to say one wants a free and equal South Africa. The shift in "context" offers a different way of thinking about and acting upon the problem. It says that the best solution won't simply be implementing the desired changes of equal opportunity (a content change) but in changing the way people participate in the process (a context shift). It requires a new way of seeing the problem, a different way of thinking about it and a new way of acting, versus simply accomplishing the goal in the old environment.

The old environment, or context, alone would never have supported the fundamentally new country that South Africa has become. The new context led to more than policy changes, but to an entirely new government, a brand new constitution, and a fresh approach to creating a free and united country in the late 20th century. Every citizen was invited to participate by submitting suggestions for the new constitution. Every person had a voice in the creation of the new political context.

Taking a Stand

Taking a stand, a characteristic of the intentional model, is quite different than producing consensus. Dualistic, black-and-white thinking about what's useful and what's not, typical of the past-oriented traditional model, generally does not serve an intentional leader. Taking a stand means that the power to lead comes from within, that it is "self-referral." This concept of self-reference says that the goals, the focus, and the intention is not based on things from the outside (known as object-reference), the most common reference point. Rather it is based upon a sense of "knowing" the direction and a clear sense of "believing" that the outcome, the vision and the intention is possible (even if everyone else thinks it's impossible).

You've got to stand for something or
you'll fall for anything.
– Aaron Tippin, as sung in
"You've Got to Stand for Something"

On May 25, 1961, John F. Kennedy, President of the United States, presented a bold challenge before a joint session of Congress. His challenge was to send a man to the moon by the end of the decade. Some thought Kennedy a lunatic; others viewed the challenge as a strategic move in the growing Cold War with the Soviet Union. Here are his words spoken on this date in history: "I believe that this nation should commit itself to achieving the goal, before this decade is out, of landing a man on the moon and returning him safely to the Earth."

Prior to his statement, Kennedy had researched this idea, determining that safely landing a man on the moon would be technologically daunting, but it was a goal that the United States could reach before the Soviet Union as the Soviets had been first to send a satellite into space, Sputnik, and four years later the first to send a man into space, cosmonaut Yuri Gagarin. "No single space project in this period will be more impressive to mankind, or more important for the long-range exploration of space; and none will be so difficult or expensive to accomplish," Kennedy said.

As opposed to sticking to a "position," taking a "stand" is more flexible. The difference is in requiring a certain solution to send a man to the moon versus setting the intention of sending a man to the moon, and then releasing the "mechanism" for its fulfillment, or how it would happen, to others who became inspired by Kennedy's vision. Once others were "enrolled" in his vision, they would then play the intention-mechanism game for real, until a viable solution was found.

The difference is like that between a brick wall and a weeping willow tree. One is fixed and unmovable, no matter what (a position). The other (a stand), the flexible tree, is firmly rooted yet sways with the wind. The tree is much better able to handle a high wind, a strong storm or an earthquake than is the brick wall. A stand holds onto the core principles, its "roots", and allows the tree to sway in the winds of life adapting to changing approaches yet maintaining strong principles and a clear vision.

'Cause when push comes to shove
You taste what your made of
You might bend 'til you break
'Cause it's all you can take
On your knees you look up
Decide you've had enough
You get mad, you get strong
Wipe you hands, shake it off
Then you stand, then you stand.
– Rascal Flatts, as sung in "Stand"

A stand is specifically not about trying to make everybody happy or trying to be accepted by everyone (the downside of consensus-building) but rather staying true to your ideals. It's not about winning people over by coercion or compromise but rather by creating a compelling vision that inspires and enrolls others to participate by choice. Rather than placing attention upon what people think of you, it's about focusing attention on how can you manifest the vision, staying positive and open to the possibilities. It's valuable to remember that much of what exists in our world today was once believed by many to be impossible. A stand is knowing that before long, "evidence" of your vision will manifest and prove the validity of your intention. It is about belief, trust and faith in your intention!

Creating New Possibilities

Beyond the traditional model of reaching goals that correspond to a vision based on reaching consensus, intentional creation opens up new possibilities. Accomplishing goals and creating desired outcomes is indeed a core part of intentional leadership, however it is done not simply by manifesting new material objects in the world. It is done by opening up new approaches and ideas for how the desired changes can appear in the world. It is staying open and attuned to new paradigms, or contexts for success. It includes rational thought, but also incorporates intuitive guidance and effective collaboration as a basis for new solutions. It is about honoring both logical reasoning and "gut feel."

Making Bold Promises

How many people play life safely? I'm not suggesting recklessness in one's approach to life but rather to consciously take appropriate risks. Most people are overcome by fear, especially in the workplace, when it comes to commitment. Therefore most people tend to make feasible promises that they can be counted on to keep. They don't rock the boat or take too many chances.

Be bold. Be clear. Believe in yourself.
– Marc Carignan

However, it is by taking selected risks that people produce new break-throughs for success. Being bold about what might be possible, trying out new approaches, or investigating new ideas brings much excitement and often unforeseen benefits. To go down this path of creating new successes often requires making bold promises, to yourself and others. These may in fact be promises that you may not know exactly how to keep. Such bold promises become personal commitments that can drive you to new level of originality and creativity. Kennedy certainly demonstrated that he knew about making bold promises when he challenged America to send a man to the moon!

Making bold commitments is about daring to be great and furthermore, planning to be great! It's easy to get what others have in their lives: do what they do. People who have created great success in the world have thought and acted in ways that most people were unwilling to think or act.

Nelson Mandela did not know the details about how his vision would be implemented. Until the vision unfolded in a series of dramatic episodes in late 20th century South African history, he did not know which mechanisms would cause his intended results. He was bold in his promises that South Africa would become free and his commitment was to persist until this vision became reality.

When your vision is clear and compelling, bold promises actually cause Universal forces to come to your aid. People, ideas, and circumstances tend to become attracted to you in ways that were previously unseen. This played out on a large scale and quite dramatically in the re-birth of the nation of South Africa, especially as much of the world participated economically and politically to pressure the country to abandon the policy of apartheid, a policy similar to the one the US had previously utilized with the concept of "separate but equal" justice. Remember that large, "impossible" visions inspire people more than smaller ones. Since it costs no more to dream big than to dream small, and since big dreams and visions inspire more people and enroll others into your way of thinking, why not dream big?

If you are going to think, think big.
– Donald Trump

Acting from the Future

Finally, intentional leaders act from the future with the vision of the way it will be in the future clear in their minds. They have a clear vision of not just what they want to create but how it will be once it has been created. They consider how it will feel once it becomes a reality and what new thinking may originate from that future place. These leaders act as if it has already happened, that its outcome is a certainty. They operate in the present with the knowledge that the future vision must and will manifest. They hold a vision so compelling and clear that it is only a matter of time and persistence before it shows up. They allow the Universe to manifest the desire with the flexibility and trust that there are many ways in which the vision could manifest.

The traditional approach of reacting from past experiences and the way things have been done before is an approach based on the past. It ignores in large part what might be possible from the present going forward. It is limiting as it expects and almost requires a "repeat performance" of the way things have occurred previously. It does not easily allow new and flexible approaches to achieve the goals, approaches which may be faster, better and more beneficial overall.

Intentional leaders remain open and willing to have their vision become a reality in whatever way they are guided to proceed, along with the people who are attracted to and enrolled by their vision. They stay open to and aware of new ideas and opportunities that appear along the way to guide them to their ultimate goal. They stay open to inspiration and intuition and take corresponding actions that are in alignment with such thoughts. They stay true to their principles and to their codes of honor. They remember that life is not simply about reaching their goals but in walking the path towards their goals while fully experiencing life.

Why Lead by Intention?

Why would you want to lead by intention? It seems that the traditional leadership techniques are well ingrained in western societies. Why buck the system? Traditional approaches seem to work, don't they? The answer is simple. In fact, the answer to that question is the same as the answer to the following question: What are the costs of the "struggle" and "constant competition" that the traditional leadership model requires?

Leading by intention operates in a context of flexibility, openness and "flow." This flow is connected to the flow of life in the Universe. Grass does not struggle to grow, it just grows. It does so easily and effortlessly, according to design. Birds don't try to fly, they fly. When you tap into your intuition alongside rational thought (rather than rational thought alone), you are also in the flow of things. We are part of the natural order of the world, just like grass and birds.

We need not try to be successful. We need only choose to be successful, and we can do so by our own definition. This is living in the flow. This is the life of an intentional leader.

The Power of Attraction

When you are drawing from the infinite, you can never take more than your share. Abundance is your birthright.
– Thomas Troward, a late 19th century teacher of Mental Science and direct contributor to Science of Mind (Religious Science) teachings, influencing Ernest Holmes, Emmett Fox and others

What Do You Want to Create?

As mentioned earlier, the Law of Attraction is one of the most powerful laws in the Universe. It states that "like attracts like." Since everything in the world is composed of energy, as the first Universal Law states, it follows that energy attracts other energy like itself, that the vibration of the sender's energy will match the vibration of the energy received, or what is attracted to them.

Think of your car radio for a moment. Would you tune your radio to 690 AM and expect to receive the signal being broadcast on 91.1 FM? Of course you wouldn't. You must set the radio dial to 91.1 FM in order to receive the signal being broadcast on that frequency. This is the way all energy vibration works, not just with radio waves.

The way humans vibrate energetically is through our thoughts and the corresponding emotional feelings that we experience. Stop for a moment to consider these questions. What do you think about most of the time? What are your dominant thoughts? You see, your mind is always focused on something.

What have you been thinking about most? Are you thinking primarily about what you want or more about what you don't want? The evidence is all around you. For most of us, it is a mixture of things that we consider to be good and those we consider to be bad (or at least less desirable). Your external world is a reflection of your inner world. Put another way, what is manifesting in the physical world – money, career, relationships, health, and so on – is a reflection of what is happening inside of you, with your thoughts and feelings.

Most people focus the majority of their thoughts on "current reality", on what has already manifested. They focus their attention on the things currently in their world, such as the money in their bank account, their relationships and their health, whether good or bad. When people offer the majority of their thought on current reality, their thoughts tend to go to the negative. People seem more likely to think statements like, "I sure hope I don't get laid off at work," "I don't want to get cancer like that guy on TV," or "I'll probably never lose all this baby fat no matter how hard I try." Negative or hopeless thoughts create corresponding negative or hopeless feelings. Appreciative and hopeful thoughts create corresponding feelings too. It's really very simple. That's not to say that negative people don't experience some happiness but for many people, their dominant thoughts are about lack or scarcity, or about what they don't want in their lives or in the world.

Your Unconscious Mind Cannot Negate

Your unconscious mind knows nothing about wanting one thing or not wanting another. That is, your mind cannot "negate" a thought, such as in saying "I don't want to be fat." It is actually more powerful to say, "I want to be fit and healthy," stating it in the affirmative. This isn't just about positive thinking either.

The reason for this is that your unconscious mind thinks only in pictures, or concepts. There's no way for your mind to think about a negated concept such as "not fat" as your mind has to conjure up "fat" first, and hence you vibrate with "fat," whether you want it or not. As we live in a vibrational world, when you think fat, wanting it or not wanting it, you are "vibrating" fat. The vibrations of our unconscious mind are "additive" meaning that it is a combination of everything you think about. What you think about, you vibrate. What you vibrate, you also attract.

It's also the same with money thoughts. It's better to think "I want to be financially prosperous" rather than "I want to get out of debt" – even if it's true that you want to get out of debt. You see, regardless of whether your conscious mind is thinking "get out of debt" or "get into debt," your unconscious mind pictures and hence vibrates "debt." Because like energies attract, you actually tend to attract more debt when you think this way, regardless of whether you're thinking "get out" or "get in" with regards to the debt.

This strategy is not about ignoring the reality outright so much as it's about focusing on the desired state. For example, if you are in debt, set up a debt re-payment plan and then remove your attention from debt and focus on building financial prosperity. If you are fat, stop weighing your body every-day and complaining about being fat. Focus instead on healthy eating and exercise habits, those behaviors that fit and healthy people follow. Focus on your desire to be fit and healthy, rather than focusing on avoiding being fat.

Leading On a Larger Scale

As a leader, it is important for you to consider the concept of attraction on a larger scale as well, especially as you consider the influence that attraction has on others and on the world at large. You see, popular US concepts today such as the "war on terror" and the "war on drugs" have actually done nothing to reduce or eliminate these problems. In fact, continued focus on these negative, or negated, concepts have caused these problems to grow. There is more terror and there are more drugs in the US and in the world than ever before. This constant "negative" focus has created a sense of constant, draining fear in many people. There's no doubt that terrorism and drugs have had a negative influence on people in the world, the rule of law, and the hope for peace and civility. However, the solution is not to fight against them, but rather to focus on the desired outcome.

Let's focus on peace, safety and respect in the world. All outer changes in the world begin as inner changes. Just as all great works of art started within the artists who created them, all great missions of peace and hope in the world start with a personal experience of inner peace and hope. Each one of us can begin this transformation within ourselves today. The truth of the matter is that you cannot have peace outside if you don't have peace on the inside.

What we resist persists.
– Carl Jung

Here's a bold, intentional leadership idea. Rather than thinking about a "war on terror", let's choose a more empowering focus such as a "commitment to peace." Rather than the United States using the Department of Defense to enforce the US point of view in the world and the Department of Homeland Security to protect us in a world cloaked with fear and suspicion and eroding personal freedoms, let's create a new department. Let's create the "Department of Peace." This peace department would be tasked with creating an honest and intentional dialogue with the world community, relegating the DOD and DOHS to true defensive roles rather than the offensive postures they have embodied in the US and in the world today.

A Department of Peace is an approach that every major world tradition and religion could support. This is not a partisan concept, but a human concept. This is also a secular concept, one that would ultimately shift our focus from fear and a concept of the world as evil to a focus on peace for all people. This focus would shift from the current conversation of "why we can't" create peace to the more powerful conversation of "how we can" create it.

In committed discussions and with an intention to create world peace, we could release the idea that war can actually achieve our goals of domestic security. Ultimately, most of us realize that war against an often unseen enemy cannot guarantee our safety. Education, trust and a focus on the desired state – peace – would begin to shift the world energy. The US has an opportunity to take a brave, bold step in leading the world, not by harassment but by true leadership, by proposing bold measures and initiatives to once and for all create peace on our planet. It all starts with intention and leaders with the courage to take such a stand!

I'm not suggesting that the DOD or DOHS are not required in today's world; I believe that they still are. What I am suggesting is a new strategy and a new context. I suggest focusing on the desired state, beginning to feel what a peaceful and loving world would truly be like, and taking actions that are consistent with that desire. Be clear on the intention and be willing to try out various mechanisms to achieve peace!

Mother Teresa was asked years ago if she would participate in an anti-war rally. She declined saying that she would not participate in an anti-war event, but said if they held a march for peace, she would attend. She understood the energy that she projected would return to her. She understood "like attracts like." She understood the Law of Attraction.

The Emotional Guidance Scale

Now that we've discussed "thinking" in detail, let's focus now on our emotions, the "feelings" we experience. Our feelings can be measured along a scale called the Emotional Guidance Scale, as described by Esther and Jerry Hicks in their book, "Ask and It Is Given." They teach that our current emotions are an indication of our current "vibration." As masters in using the Law of Attraction, they explain that how you "feel" – whether it's depression, anger, boredom, joy and so on – is a signal to you about what you are thinking.

It would be impossible to scan every thought you have throughout the day, which some experts have estimated at 60,000 or more. What you can notice, especially as you become more aware and pay greater attention, is how you are feeling in any given moment. Are you at peace? Anxious? Scared? Bored? Confused? Lost? Trapped? Happy? Joyful? Feeling a sense a freedom? Or love?

How you are feeling is an indication of your dominant thoughts. As you begin to notice your emotional states, I invite you not to judge them. We all experience a whole range of human emotions sometimes in a single day! Your feelings are a kind of "short hand" notation for the complexity of thoughts you have moment to moment. They are the emotional "summary" of your thoughts.

When you are in vibrational alignment, you feel good feelings. You feel happy and joyful. You feel free and loving. Life is good. When you are out of alignment, you feel the feelings we call "bad feelings." You feel frustrated, angry, rageful or depressed. With that said, "check in" with yourself right now. What are you feeling in this moment?

What is it then to be in "vibrational alignment?" Simply put, it is the alignment of your dominant thoughts and the life you truly desire. This is not to say that you will never feel any of the bad feelings. It is that when you are in alignment, the dominant emotional state you experience is that of peace, joy, appreciation, love and bliss.

Most of us have had glimpses of these experiences, most notably when we first fall in love. When you do pursue what you truly want or what you are most passionate about you come into alignment. In its simplest form, that is all that is required to be happy!

Your vibration, whether good or bad, causes people, ideas and opportunities that vibrate likewise to be attracted to you. So if you are feeling predominantly unhappy, dissatisfied and frustrated, you will tend to attract people who complain of the same things and have similar thoughts and feelings of unhappiness, dissatisfaction and frustration. When you are optimistic and focused on "how" you might create your ideal situation, and begin taking substantial steps in that direction, you shift your vibration toward more happiness, greater satisfaction and even patience with the process. From this place, you attract people that can help you accelerate your journey, more positive people who want to help you. You attract more powerful ideas at that higher vibration as well, much like tuning your radio dial to a higher frequency and picking up the music being broadcast at that frequency. You attract opportunities you might have passed by previously when you were vibrating at the lower, negative vibrations.

The Emotional Guidance System model is actually a simple linear scale of emotional states, ranging from fear and depression at the lowest vibrational levels of the scale to love, joy and appreciation at the highest levels. Most of us spend the majority of our time in between these extremes. There are many emotional states we can feel and this list is a good approximation of the major emotions we experience, listed in descending vibrational order.

Emotional Guidance Scale

The following list is taken from the book, *Ask and It Is Given*, by Esther and Jerry Hicks, based on the teachings of Abraham:

1. Joy / Knowledge / Empowerment / Freedom / Love / Appreciation
2. Passion
3. Enthusiasm / Eagerness / Happiness
4. Positive Expectation / Belief
5. Optimism
6. Hopefulness
7. Contentment
8. Boredom
9. Pessimism
10. Frustration / Irritation / Impatience
11. "Overwhelment"

12. Disappointment

13. Doubt

14. Worry

15. Blame

16. Discouragement

17. Anger

18. Revenge

19. Hatred / Rage

20. Jealousy

21. Insecurity / Guilt / Unworthiness

22. Fear / Grief / Depression / Despair / Powerlessness

The higher the vibration, the more positive the emotion. Whatever you call the emotion, the truth is this: the better you feel, the more in alignment you are. The more in alignment you are, the more likely that your desires will manifest quickly and easily.

When you change the way you look at things,
the things you look at change.
– Wayne Dyer

Your work, therefore, is first to get clear about what you want. Then get into vibrational alignment with that desire. You don't need to know every step that you'll need to take in order to start. You don't need to do it all by yourself either. Remember that Universal Laws will play a large part in manifesting your intention.

Envision what is would be like to really reach your goals and what it would feel like upon achieving success. It's not just about taking different action (the content) but it's about shifting the "context" of your thinking and your life to match your desire. It is also not about trying to change or control external things, events or people to conform to your desires. When you lead by intention, changing the context within you is the most powerful approach for creating your ideal life and your desired outcomes in all areas.

Boldness and Positive Expectations

Those who dare to fail miserably
can achieve greatly.
– John F. Kennedy

What Do You Expect?

It is imperative that you become clear about what you want, that you take action you are inspired to take, and that you have positive expectations about actually achieving your goals. (We will discuss inspired action in a later chapter.)

Think about the last time you placed an order at your favorite restaurant. After deciding what you wanted for your meal, you placed your order with the waiter. When you placed your order, did you expect to receive what you ordered when the meal arrived? Of course you did! We don't place orders at restaurants expecting the wrong thing to show up at our table. (If we are planning for the wrong order to arrive, we may want to find a new, more reliable restaurant.) We place our order, expecting that what we have selected will arrive. If it does not arrive properly, we then take some corresponding action such as sending back the meal to have it corrected. The fact remains, however, that we expect the meal to arrive as ordered. That is our intention.

Boldly going forward and asking for what you want is similar to ordering at a restaurant and expecting a certain outcome. Notice that when you placed your restaurant order you didn't specify all the details that the kitchen and wait staff should perform in order for your meal to arrive as specified. You specified your order then released the details of preparing and serving your meal to the waiter and other restaurant staff. You expected and trusted in the proper performance of their responsibilities.

You'll never know how far you can go unless
you're willing to go too far.
– Lifespring mantra

Unless you associate with mind readers, people really don't know what you want unless you ask. Asking for what you want is powerful and is only possible if you are clear about what you want. As for creating the results you want in your life, remember that you don't need to do everything yourself. Wouldn't you like your desires to come about faster and easier? Then give others the opportunity to help you. Allow the Universal Laws to support you. Work in alignment with these natural laws, rather than attempting to fight them.

The Art of Allowing

Finally, for attraction to work you must "allow" the results of your intentions to come to you. If you are thinking that the outcome is unlikely, or that you probably don't deserve it, or that it's going to take a long time, then it probably will. It can become a self-fulfilling prophecy, delaying what you desire. It's as much an art as a science to allow the "good" to flow into your life. The science is the Law of Attraction and other Universal Laws. The art is the practicing of these principles, the awareness of what you are feeling, and the refocusing of your thoughts as required to keep them focused on the desired outcome. You must "step into the future" in your mind, visioning your desired results. (We will discuss vision shortly).

As Aladdin's genie always said, "Your wish is my command." If you say you don't deserve it, the genie will comply. If you say it's going to take a long time, the genie will comply. However, if you say you deserve good things because you desire a good life with wonderful people and fabulous things in it, the genie will also comply – if you allow it.

This is not to say that the genie "really exists." It is, however, a powerful paradigm, or story, that implies that you set yourself up for success or failure in your life based upon your thinking and your corresponding feelings on the matter.

You've got to be clear. You've got to be consistent. You also have to allow the good to come into your life. Remind yourself that you are as worthy as everyone else on this planet. You deserve to manifest a wonderful life. Be bold and ask for what you want. Although your intentions will usually require some action on your part, you must first and foremost prepare your thoughts for the outcome you desire. Once you gain mastery over your dominant thoughts and their corresponding emotions, you will attract all you desire to you.

Leadership

Intention

Vision

Practice

Confidence

Attitude

Learning

Chapter 3. Vision Creates Clarity in Your Life

Imagining Your Desires

Imagination is more important
than knowledge.
– Albert Einstein

What is Your Vision?

What have you imagined yourself creating or having in your life? Perhaps you have imagined financial freedom, relationship happiness, physical vitality, the pursuit of worthwhile intellectual activities, a growing enlightenment or the raising of your consciousness? If you have, you are really on a powerful path!

Have you imagined abundance in some or all of areas of your life? Have you considered what "legacy" you want to leave behind, financially or otherwise? That is, what do you want to leave behind in money and in personal, community or societal impact as a "footprint" of your life on this planet?

Vision is imagining clearly what you want and how it would look. As we learned when reviewing the importance of intention, the least important aspect is the mechanism, or how you will actually create your desires. It is the vision that defines the outcome of the intention. It describes how the end result will "look" when it is achieved. However, you have to know what you want and why you want it.

Clarity is Power

He who is most clear wins!
– John Demartini, inspirational speaker and
creator of the self-help methodology, The
Demartini Method®

Clarity is Knowing the Outcome You Expect

Whoever has more clarity in a situation wins the "game." If I am more clear about an outcome that I desire than you are in a negotiation, for example, I am far more likely to succeed in achieving my intention. There's a powerful Chinese proverb that goes, "If you don't know where you're going, any road will do." Clarity is about knowing what you want and where you're going.

This brings up the primary question that you must ask yourself, "What do I want?" Put another way, ask yourself, "What is my desired outcome?" Many people really don't know, or have focused on so many other things for so long that they have forgotten what they truly want in their lives. Or perhaps what they want is simply something like "more money" or "a better career."

Most people find it much easier to get clear about what they don't want than what they do. Don't fight it. A "don't want" list is a great starting point for getting to what you do want!

Contrast With What You Don't Want

Here's an easy exercise that I learned from Jack Canfield, co-creator of the book series "Chicken Soup for the Soul," that will help bring clarity to what you really want. If you are clear about what you want in all of your life areas (including financial, relational, intellectual, physical and spiritual) then there's no need for this exercise. However I find that most people have one or more areas that could use further clarification.

Take a blank sheet of paper and draw a vertical line down the center of the page. At the top of the left hand column, write "What I Don't Want". At the top of the right column, write "What I Do Want". Now, as quickly as you can and without thinking too hard, write a list in the left hand column of only the things you do not want in your life. If you run out of space, simply create another page, writing only in the left hand column. Leave the right hand columns on all pages blank for now.

Here are some examples of what you may not want, in various life areas. First, things you may not want financially are:

- I don't want to be broke.
- I'm tired of living paycheck to paycheck.
- I really wouldn't want to be homeless.

Let's look at some unwanted relational ideas:

- I don't want to be alone.
- I don't want to grow old by myself.
- I really don't like people who try to control me.

Unwanted intellectual ideas might include:

- I don't like my job.
- I don't feel like I'm pursuing what I really care about in life.
- I dislike not having the time or energy to pursue my hobbies.

Physically unwanted ideas include:

- I really don't want to be fat anymore.
- I don't like feeling so tired and exhausted after work every day.
- I hope I don't get cancer or some other disease.

And finally, unwanted spiritual ideas could be:

- I don't like it when I'm so hard on myself.
- I hate it when I overreact over the little things that go wrong in my life.
- I don't want to feel so alone in the world.

Getting To What You Want

You're welcome to use any of these ideas as you build your own list. Once you've completed your list, then go back to the top of the list on the first page. Reading through your list of dislikes, and to the right of each, write the "exact opposite" in the right hand column. The exact opposite can then be used as the basis for what you do want! It's OK to write more than one opposite statement in the right hand column for each item in the left, as there may be different aspects of turning the negative into a positive that you would like to express. The goal is simply to turn the negative into a related positive statement or two!

Let's look at a few examples for our "don't want" list above:

WHAT I DON'T WANT	WHAT I DO WANT
I don't want to be broke.	I want to be financially independent.
	I want to be responsible for my own financial destiny.
I don't like my job.	I want to work for a company that pays me well.
	I want to work for a manager that respects and appreciates me.
	I want to create a business that I would love to pursue in my life.
I really don't want to be fat anymore.	I want a fit, vital and healthy body.
I don't like it when I'm so hard on myself.	I want to treat myself with patience, love and respect.

Treat this as a game and have fun creating these lists. This is a great way to better understand what you would like to have in your life. In your daily contrasting experiences about what you don't like or don't want, you create preferences about how you want your life to be. As you get clearer about these preferences, you'll know more clearly what choices to make in your life that will bring you maximum happiness.

The pain pushes you until the vision pulls you.
– Michael Beckwith

You're presented with choices everyday. You may not always see the opportunities that surround you, but the clearer you are about what you want, the more likely that you'll see the options presented to you daily more as opportunities than as challenges. These are opportunities to make choices that support what you truly want, things that you are truly clear about creating in your life. Use this exercise to get clear about what's important to you. When you do, your choices in life become simpler because you know immediately if you are being presented with an "opportunity" that you will like, or not.

Visualizing Techniques

Create a Vision Board

Now that you know what you want, now's the time to create a Vision Board. There are many ways to create one, from cutting out pictures and headlines from various magazines to writing your desires on sticky notes. Let's look at these two techniques.

First, a picture-oriented Vision Board is usually done on a large piece of poster board. You'll need a stack of magazines (old magazines are just fine), poster board, glue or tape, a pair of scissors and your imagination. Also, think about what you want and bring an attitude of fun and creativity!

Start reading through each magazine you choose, cutting out the pictures, diagrams, headlines or whatever else speaks to your desires or your wants. Select cutouts that express the range of the things you desire, such as pictures of money or wealth or the things you can acquire with wealth like new cars and houses. Cut out pictures of fit and healthy bodies, great relationships and so on. Also cut out any headlines or phrases that further define your desires.

Once you've cut out a stack of pictures and headlines, arrange them on the board however you choose. Many people group things by category such as positioning the physical health pictures in one area and the financial wealth pictures in another. Once you like the layout, start taping or gluing the bits of cutout paper. There's no right or wrong way to do this exercise. Paste the cutouts any way you choose. Let it express you. Once you have completed this board, post it where you can see it everyday, either in your home or your office. A bedroom or home office space is ideal for many people.

Then look at your board everyday and imagine those things as already in your life. Rather than looking at it and feeling a "wanting," or a sense of "not having" it, get into the feeling of what it will be like when you truly have these things in your life. Move from the "wanting" feelings to "having" feelings, or sensing what it will be like to have these things in your life. Try it.

Look at your completed board, breathe deeply, and then close your eyes and imagine yourself in the scenes you've created, scenes of wealth, health and happiness. When I say "imagine yourself in the scenes," I do not mean that you should see yourself as a character in the pictures. Many people do it this way and this does not work very well. What really works is to "stay in your own body" while imagining the scenes. See the scenes as if you are a part of the action. Whether you are imaging still pictures or a movie, be a part of the scene. Feel it. Walk around in it. Enjoy it!

This process is quick, taking only a few minutes each day, feels great and sets in motion unconscious attraction that will astound you! You will begin to attract everything you need, people, things and ideas, that will make your desires a reality.

It just takes one idea to live like a king for the rest of your life.
– Ross Perot

Sticky Note Board

A variation is the sticky note vision board. This approach requires one or more stacks of sticky notes (I like 3" x 3" multi-colored ones), thin felt markers, and a poster board. Simply write one or more words on each sticky note describing something you want, whether it's related to your state of being, what you want to be doing, or what you'd like to have. For example, some things I've written in the past are items like:

- Be a Courageous Person (a "being" desire)
- Vacation in Peru (a "doing" desire)
- Live in a Beachfront House (a "having" desire)

These are examples of "being," "doing" and "having" desires. Stick the notes anywhere on the poster board. You can also write directly on the board, drawing shapes or writing messages that tie together all the notes you've stuck on the board.

Once you've written down the things you want onto the notes and have stuck them on the boards, you can rearrange them into whatever groupings make sense to you, such as groups relating to career, family, money or relationships. When I've done this, I've used some sticky notes to list the categories as well, such as notes that say "Financial," "Relational," and "Physical." Then I've arranged the related sticky notes around each of these categories as a way to organize the layout. You simply choose the layout that works best for you.

This board then becomes a basis for the actions, or goals, that you will plan to take in your life. (We'll discuss action in a later chapter.) If you need to be reminded of what you truly want, take a look at this board for guidance and to get a sense of how it will "feel" to get what you want in your life. Follow the same steps for visualizing with the board as described above in the Vision Board section. And have fun with it!

Vision with All Your Senses

What does it mean to "vision" with all your senses? It means that to strengthen a vision, you can supplement the images you are creating in your mind by tapping into your non-visual senses. When you vision or imagine, don't just "look" at the pictures or movies in your imagination. Sense them with your various physical senses!

Ask yourself questions that encourage you to feel how your body is responding to the images. You may even want to write your sensory experiences on paper. In NLP (Neuro-Linguistic Programming), there is an acronym that is used to refer to the five senses, written VAKOG. This stands for the Visual, Auditory, Kinesthetic, Olfactory and Gustatory modalities, or what you see, hear, feel, smell and taste, respectively. Here are some example questions to elicit various sensory experiences of your "vision":

Visual Questions

- What does it look like?
- How bright is it?
- What colors do you see?

Auditory Questions

- What does it sound like?
- What can you hear?
- What music is playing?

Kinesthetic Questions

- How does it feel?

- What's the weather in the scene?
- How comfortable is it for you to be there?

Olfactory Questions

- What smells do you notice?
- Is there a dominant scent or fragrance?
- Are you noticing any usual smells?

Gustatory Question

- What does it taste like?
- Is it sweet, salty or spicy?
- What's most delicious about your vision?

Of course, there are thousands of other questions you could also use but these are great questions to get you started. Using your other physical senses, or modalities as NLP refers to them, strengthens the experience of your visions. You become clearer and your mind starts believing that the desired vision is already occurring. People tend to prefer one of these modalities over the others. In fact, most people prefer visual as their dominant way of experiencing the world. However, there are also millions of people who prefer auditory or kinesthetic experiences as their most powerful way to experience the world.

Based on scientific evidence about the workings of the mind, it has been shown that the unconscious mind cannot tell the difference between reality, as reported by your senses, and a strong imagination, such as a powerful vision that you focus upon with clarity and belief. In the 1980s and 1990s, Denis Waitley implemented what he called "Visual Motor Rehearsal" into the US Olympics program. VMR was used to train Olympic athletes by tapping into the power of their unconscious minds. Researchers were able to measure brain wave and physical response activity and noticed that when athletes actively focused their minds and ran their events "in their minds," their bodies exhibited similar physiological responses as the real events. That is, their bodies responded with twitching muscles, increased heart rates, greater oxygen uptake, and more.

In practicing this technique, the athletes felt like they were competing in the events. They imagined not just running the race, but winning it. They saw themselves running their events, winning them and then receiving the gold medal on stage. Because of the Law of Attraction, they began to cause the attraction of the people, places and things required to create their desired outcome – winning the gold medal. What is the "gold medal" you'd like to achieve in your life?

There are those who look at things the way
they are, and ask why... I dream of things that
never were, and ask why not?
– Robert "Bobby" Kennedy, US politician;
candidate for 1968 US presidential election;
assassinated during run for president;
brother of John F. Kennedy

Why Visualize?

Why should you visualize anyway? Why not just go off and take action? Why "waste" time thinking about what you want, writing about it, feeling it in your body, and so on? The reasons are twofold.

First, as we discussed earlier, it is important for you to get clear. The clearer you are, the more certain you will be as you walk your path. The more certain you are, the more you will know which choice you should make when the road forks in front of you. You will feel clearer about which decision you should make when presented with various choices.

Secondly, visualize to simply "feel good." This may sound simplistic and even trivial, but I assure you that it is extremely important. The human condition is always about contrast. It's about what feels good and what doesn't. It always seems to come down to this simple distinction.

Therefore, visualize to feel good! Visualize in order to experience the emotional states that you want to experience. Everything that you want in the world, whether it's "being" something, "doing" something, or "having" something, comes down to the emotional states you want to experience in being, doing or having the "thing" you desire. No one wants to be rich so that they'll have more colored paper in their wallet! They want to be rich because of the perceived way it will make them feel when they can buy what they want, or contribute to causes that interest them, or help friends or family in need. It's about how the money will make us feel. It's our perception of the emotions that will accompany having the money! This concept is true for every want.

Everything we want is about getting to a desired emotion or "feeling state." Therefore, you can visualize achieving a better feeling state even if you don't actually have the things you want yet in your life. You can begin to "close the gap" in your emotional states, experiencing better and better feelings, even before getting the actual things that you desire in your physical experience. Closing this gap sets the unconscious mind in rapid motion to cause the physical to appear, to see opportunities and seize ideas that you would otherwise miss or ignore. When you start feeling good, as if you have the money or relationships you truly want, then those things appear!

Feeling good is the great motivator. Visualize every day to feel good! Tap into the "feel good pharmacy" in your brain. It is better than any anti-depressant or mood-elevator you could ever experience, and it's there anytime you want it. Remember, the things you think about the most become your reality!

Passion and Purpose

When the voice and the vision on the inside become more profound, and more clear and loud than the opinions on the outside, you've mastered your life.
– John Demartini

Your Passion Will Drive You

What are you passionate about? What are you here to do with your life? What legacy would be worthy of you? What do you value most in the world? These questions can support you in clarifying your "purpose." All great leaders in the world have claimed a purpose in their lives, often called their "personal mission." Personal mission statements are a great clarifying tool in getting your ideas onto paper. I've noticed in my life that when I write things down that they feel more "real" to me and doing so frees my mind from having to keep "remembering" them. Things become more real to me while my mind becomes more relaxed.

When writing your personal mission statement, you can write it to be very specific or broader in focus. A mission statement acts as an "invisible hand" to help guide your actions to align yourself with what you really want and care about most.

Here are some examples of personal mission statements:

- My purpose is to embrace my life and to make a difference in other people's lives by sharing my love and my gifts with the world.

- I am an optimist and enjoy everything I do and all that I experience in life. I am known by my family as a woman who loves and cares; by my friends as someone who is always there; by my employers as a fair, honest, responsible and hardworking individual. I believe that every action I take and every thought I have is directed by my values and my sense of integrity. I choose to live a life without regrets.

- My mission is to be true to my values of love, courage, and appreciation. I choose to be an example of love in action, a model for the power of love, and loving even when it's difficult. I am courageous, willing to step into the unknown and past my fear in pursuit of worthy goals and ideas. I live in appreciation for all that I have, all that I do, and all I have become in the world. I appreciate others for their magnificence within and appreciate my opportunity, however brief, to make a difference with my presence and by my stand in the world.

Create a Personal Mission Statement

What's your inspiring personal mission? Were you inspired by or did you relate to any of the examples above? Writing a personal mission statement invites you to think more deeply about your life, clarifying what's most important to you. Your mission doesn't have to look anything like the ones above. It simply needs to express what moves you, what is most important to you.

Writing it down and keeping it brief encourages you to be clear and succinct. It actually takes more time and focus to keep it short and to the point, but it is worth the effort because it leads to more clarity as well. As John Demartini says, "He who is most clear, wins." He, or she, who is most clear gets what they truly want in life!

Do what you love, or find something you do.
Life's too short to spend your time on things
that don't bring you joy and happiness.
– Marc Carignan

As you define your mission, you get to claim more clearly and firmly this statement as your own. Rather than just generally thinking about what you want, you then have a concrete, well-defined set of concepts that you are claiming as your driving force. When you write things down, you also engage additional physical senses in writing, reading, speaking, and even hearing it. (I recorded mine in my own voice and then loaded it onto my iPod with motivational background music.)

Refer often to your mission to consciously keep these ideas in front of you as you plan the goals and actions of your life. Here are some guidelines that may help you in creating your own mission statement.

Guidelines for Creating a Personal Mission Statement

1. Consider who you want to become, what you want to do and what you want to have in your life. Life is much more than just acquiring stuff. (Ask anyone who has a lot of stuff to verify this for yourself.)

2. Consider the various roles you play in your life, or the ones you want to play. Which roles are the most important to you? Are you a parent, a citizen, a member of the community, a business owner, an employee, a green consumer, or an intentional leader? You may be all these things and more. Consider what aspects of being, doing and having relate most to your primary roles.

3. If you still need inspiration, think about one or more people that you admire in the world. What are the qualities you see in them that you most desire to embody within yourself? Consider the "being, doing and having" qualities and how they would relate to your mission statement.

4. Periodically review, evaluate and update your personal mission statement. The statement should not feel like a burden when you read it. Rather the mission should inspire you to connect to your "higher self" and bring enthusiasm and joy in reading it. Let it inspire you!

Whatever you do, have fun with this process. It isn't about getting the "right" mission statement, but creating something that excites and "juices" you, that motivates and inspires you. Creating and affirming your mission statement is as much an act of discovery as one of affirmation and commitment. It is an opportunity to go inward and remember the dreams and desires you once had but may have forgotten along the way. Remember the childhood innocence and enthusiasm for every new thing in life. This is available for you again as an adult with the right empowering mission!

I don't know how I know, but I'm gonna find my purpose. I don't know where I'm gonna look, but I'm gonna find my purpose. Got to find out, don't want to wait. Got to make sure that my life will be great. Got to find my purpose before it's too late.
– from "Avenue Q", the Broadway musical, as sung in the song, "Purpose"

The Vacation

Let's look at how our mission impacts our life experiences. As part of my mission, let's say I choose to plan a vacation. That sounds like fun. Well, I like to travel to warm climates, so let's say I decide to drive for two weeks along the highways and byways of the desert southwest of the United States. I want to visit the low deserts (including Death Valley) and the high deserts areas (including Santa Fe and Taos).

As I'm planning my trip, I realize that I'll be starting in San Diego, my home. From here I'll be driving east. Initially, I plan to drive northeast to Death Valley, then into Nevada and over into Arizona. A visit to the Grand Canyon sounds nice, then I might drive down into Phoenix and Tucson. I'll then head over to the high deserts of New Mexico, including mile-high Albuquerque and the even higher deserts of Santa Fe and Taos. Then, I'd like to come back through southern New Mexico, through Yuma, Arizona, and then through the southern part of California back to San Diego.

As I'm noticing my itinerary, I'm thinking that although I really want to visit the deserts, I'm planning to start my trip in San Diego and planning to end it there too. So, I think to myself: I could just stay home, save 2 weeks of time and money, and still arrive at my final destination: San Diego! That sounds

sounds silly, doesn't it? What happened to Phoenix, Santa Fe and the Grand Canyon?

Funny as it seems, many people seem plan their lives this way. After all, I didn't plan to go on a vacation to simply "get it done." I wanted to go for the fun, beauty and experiences along the way! This is the point of life as well. As much fun as it seems it will be to be a multi-millionaire, or fall in love with the partner of your dreams, or have a fit and healthy body, it's not just about getting to the destination. How many times have you heard people say, "I'll be happy when ..." Fill in the blank. I'll be happy when I'm rich. I'll be happy when I'm thin. I'll be happy when I'm married, or when I'm single again.

Life is not about "getting it done." It's not simply about getting everything you want. It's about experiencing the ride along the way. It's about experiencing joy and learning. To experience true joy, in fact, you have no choice but to learn and grow. The excitement is in the journey!

"Who" you become along the way, what you learn and discover about yourself and the world, and the attitude you carry along the journey are the true payoffs. Of course, you can still have the stuff you desire but do not miss out on the journey just to get the stuff. Ask anyone who has achieved material success in the world and they will say that although the stuff is good, the real joy has been in the journey, in who they've become as people, in the character they've built and in the people they have met along the way. You can still go for "the stuff" but don't do it at the expense of the experiences along the way.

Be fully engaged in your journey. Learn as much as you can. Discover what truly inspires you. It may be different than it is for others. In fact, it's likely to be different than what you read in the newspaper or see on TV. What you truly want is ultimately your own decision. Also, support others in getting what they want along the way as well. When you help others get what they want, you are much more likely to get help in getting what you want. When you arrive at the various destinations in life you will arrive more aware, more ready and more grateful for the path you have walked (or driven, flown, or even crawled) to get to your end goal.

Visions and Missions and Goals

How do visions, missions and goals work together? First, have your vision. Picture or imagine the way you'd like your life to unfold, the experiences or things you'd like to have, the people you'd like to meet, and so on. From your vision and any of the mission-building questions previously suggested, build your own personal mission statement.

Your mission should support and be in alignment with your vision. Your mission, and the vision behind it, become your purpose. They help define your reason for being here on planet Earth.

Efforts and courage are not enough without
purpose and direction.
– John F. Kennedy

Goals should be considered last. The goals are simply the action steps selected to manifest your vision. For example, a vision of being fit and healthy would have goals including daily healthy eating, regular exercise, and other healthy lifestyle choices.

The most powerful goals are measurable and have time frames attached. The question, "How many, by when?" is a useful way to think about goals. That is, each goal should be quantifiable and time-oriented. Examples are, "I will exercise 3 times a week," "I will achieve 15% body fat by December 31," or "I will climb Mt. Whitney in a single day on August 11." Use specific dates or frequencies rather than saying things like, "I will lose 15 pounds in 3 months." The problem with this is that "3 months" in the future never really comes. If you choose a date, it does. Each one of these expresses a measurable goal with a specific target date or frequency (such as "3 times a week") supporting the vision of being fit and healthy.

What's Your Trajectory?

Little changes today can make big changes later on. Try this. Draw a dot on the left side of a piece of paper. Next, draw a straight line horizontally across the page to the right edge of the page. This represents your current path, your time line. The dot is where you are today, and the line represents where you are going.

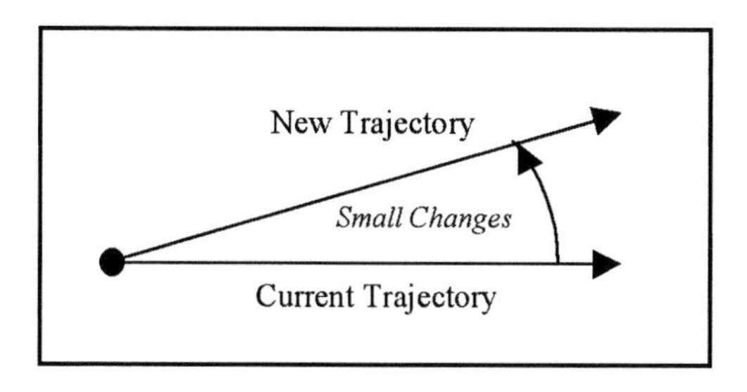

Now, place your pen back on the dot you drew. Imagining the dot as a hinge, draw another straight line, this time angled up just a little bit, again out to the right edge of the paper. Notice that the longer the line gets, the greater the distance between the original horizontal line (your current trajectory) and the new angled line (your new trajectory). Just a few degrees of change can make a big difference over time. This is the power of small changes, projected into the future.

Little hinges swing big doors.
– W. Clement Stone, a prominent 20th century businessman, philanthropist and self-help book author; co-authored the book "Success Through a Positive Mental Attitude" with Napoleon Hill

No matter the size of the door, the hinges on it are quite small in comparison. Life is often like this. Small adjustments now such as new ways of thinking, feeling and acting today can make dramatic changes in your future. All big ideas in the world start off as small ideas. All big companies in the world start off as small companies.

Disruptive Change

Do you remember your life before Microsoft? Or before Apple Computer? Do you remember your life before cellular phones? Or before television? These started out as small ideas and individual visions before becoming much larger. In each of these cases, these companies and technologies transformed the world by causing "disruptive changes" in their industries.

Change doesn't always happen smoothly and gently. Change happens in fits and turns, in little steps taken one after another. There is even an occasional gigantic change that happens, normally as a result of many smaller changes that occurred previously. Follow your vision and many things you thought would be difficult will become effortless. Some of your little ideas may even cause gigantic changes in the world. Unleash your vision today!

LEADERSHIP

INTENTION

VISION

PRACTICE

CONFIDENCE

ATTITUDE

LEARNING

Chapter 4. Mastery Requires Persistent Practice

Discipline is Overrated

You don't have to be motivated
to do what you love!
– Marc Carignan

Discipline is Not the Answer

Discipline is not the answer to achieve your goals. I know that most motivational speakers and self-help gurus like to focus on discipline. They say that it takes discipline to be great, to lose weight, to become a millionaire, and more. What if they're wrong? I'm not saying that discipline is not a useful trait. What I'm suggesting is that maybe this isn't the magic bullet that so many would like it to be!

What usually comes along with discipline is the feeling that whatever you're disciplining yourself about is not really something you want to do. This brings resistance, frustration, and requires outside motivation, with either positive or negative consequences. As the expression goes, you need to be motivated by either a carrot or a stick. There is little doubt that discipline is required to get yourself to do the things you don't really want to do. Even if you have discipline, it usually isn't long before you get tired and frustrated with "pushing" yourself everyday. Going on a diet is a great example of how people "discipline" themselves to succeed, often giving up within just a few weeks or even a few days due to the pain and frustration of pushing themselves.

This begs the question, "Why am I doing something I don't want to do?" What if there is an easier way than pushing yourself everyday? What if you don't need to kick yourself to get out of bed in the morning to exercise as you know you should? What if you get to the point where you really want to get out of bed to start your day, to live your mission, and to create the difference you want in your life and in the world? This way of living is possible, and it's a lot more fun than discipline.

Your Amazing Unconscious Mind

I believe that your success in life is not based on discipline. Your success is based primarily on your level of clarity and focus. Is what you want and what you are focusing on clearer and more compelling than the changes you will need to make to get there? Think back to the multiple ways of "visioning" with all your senses. Is what you really want more compelling, bigger and brighter to you? Can you hear the music? Do you feel what it will be like to have achieved what you desire in your life?

As humans, we often create new habits out of what we do repetitively, what we prefer, or simply what we have been trained to do. These habits, by definition, become automatic. By automatic, I am referring to the power of your unconscious mind to carry out the tasks without your conscious mind being involved. Can you imagine if you had to consciously make the tens of thousands of little decisions you make every single day? Imagine needing to orchestrate something as simple as getting out of bed, one of the first things you do every morning.

For example, to get out of bed, you need to perform the following tasks. First, you need to first move your legs. To move your legs requires contracting several of the larger muscles in your legs, and probably also requires moving muscles in your hips, back and abdomen. You then need to consider how much to squeeze each of the muscles, including the quadriceps, the gluteus maximus, the gastrocnemius and other muscles. To contract these larger muscles, you need to increase blood flow to your legs, diverting it from other areas in order to create sufficient levels of glycogen in the muscle to power the motion. Then you need to consider the amount of power to use, the distance to travel, and so on. You've only just moved your legs. There's a lot more your body has to do to get out of bed!

You absolutely require your unconscious mind to handle all the details of moving your body. This is one of its primary jobs. All your conscious mind needs to do is to decide to get out of bed and then command your body to carry out the command. Your unconscious mind then goes into action. It's a good thing that our conscious minds don't need to handle every detail or we would be exhausted before we even finished breakfast! We'd never have the conscious mental energy to get much of anything done.

Habituate Your Ways of Being and Doing

Let's get back to discussing habits. Humans have thousands of habits, many of which started as conscious step-by-step activities. Over time, these activities have become "automated" by the unconscious mind. A great example of a habit most of us have mastered is driving a car. Can you remember how scary it was when you first got behind the wheel? I remember thinking I'd love driving, but the first several times I had high levels of fear running through my mind and my body. I wondered about all the new things I had learned, the way I needed to respond to this powerful machine (the car), the rules of the road, deciding what to pay attention to while driving, staying focused, watching for pedestrians and even remembering where I was going! There really are a lot of things to remember and process.

How does it feel for you to drive today? I know it must be different from your first experience now that you have been driving for 5, 10, or perhaps even 20 years or more. For me, my unconscious mind can almost drive the car by itself. I know that today I can drive, adjust the radio, hold a conversation and talk on my mobile phone, all at the same time (although I realize that it's not recommended).

What do you think about today while driving? You probably tend to think very little of the actual driving process even while you're actually driving the car. You're likely to be a good driver despite a lack of focus on the actual driving details. Your driving habits have allowed your conscious mind to focus on "higher value activities," tasks that require more rational processing power, the domain of your conscious mind. You can decide consciously whether to bypass a certain road due to traffic, choose to take a different route, or think about what you will do when you arrive at your destination. Your unconscious mind frees up your conscious mind!

Now think about habits that don't support you as well. Do you tend to overeat, that is eating when you're not hungry or after you've just eaten? Have you done this for very long, or very frequently? Do you smoke? Of course you know that it's not a healthy choice, but you do it anyway. I'm not here to judge your choices but rather to let you know that you can change any of your habits whenever you choose. I know that's a bold statement, but it's 100% true.

There's really nothing special
about me except my choices.
– Joel Bauer, self-described "info-tainer" and
author of "How to Persuade People Who Don't
Want to Be Persuaded"

Our choices create our future. You weren't born with an overeating habit or a smoking habit. You similarly were not born with the habit of eating well and exercising daily. At some point you simply learned how to do it and began doing it repeatedly. All habits evoke in us a feeling. The habits we continue to do cause a good feeling and those habits we abandon (or never formed in the first place) cause a bad feeling.

I remember trying a few cigarettes in college. I really didn't enjoy it. I remember coughing, my throat feeling dry and scratchy, and the bad taste in my mouth the next morning. That was my experience and therefore smoking never became a habit for me. As for other people I know, they experienced something quite different and for them it did become a habit despite knowing that it was not good for them. There were other benefits for them, perhaps the stimulant effects of the nicotine, the fact that friends were doing it or the perceived "coolness" factor of smoking.

The Motivation for Our Habits

This leads us to the motivation for our habits. We choose habits for various reasons, but primarily because we believe that their outcome will produce an emotional state that we desire, such as a feeling of joy, peace or love. We may choose a positive, negative or neutral activity as a habit. Of course, these evaluations are based primarily on whether we believe these habits are good for us or not.

The truth is there are habits that you can adopt that will support you in achieving your desires. There are others that will not. As you become more aware of your habits, bringing these unconscious activities back into your conscious awareness (where they started originally), you can reconsider which support you and which do not.

The key to changing a habit is not to think of "not" doing it but to think about replacing it with a different, more supportive or powerful habit. You need a powerful reason why you want to change. You need to have a clear mental image of the more supportive habit and a powerful reason why it's important to you! When you've established this and have repeated the new behavior several times consciously, the unconscious mind will begin to learn the sequence and encode the habit into your unconscious mind, making it automatic for you. Experts have noticed that it seems to take your unconscious mind 21 days of daily, conscious repetition to make your conscious actions a habit. Therefore, you must consistently apply the power of your conscious mind for at least this long, consistently and deliberately, for your unconscious mind to take over and free you from having to think through every step of your new positive habit.

Just as heavy smokers didn't start out as two-pack-a-day users, you shouldn't expect that your new positive habits, such as exercising three times a week and eating healthy every day, will be easy at first. However, it takes only 21 days to encode the habit if you do it consistently during that time. If you have a strong enough desire for the results of the habit, then you are more likely to maintain the new habits you have developed.

Your unconscious mind takes instruction from your conscious mind about which behaviors you want to habituate to serve you in achieving your desires. Use this technique for engaging your unconscious mind to make your desired behavior, and the behavior's corresponding results, flow in your life rather than having to "discipline" yourself. Remember that you don't need to force yourself to do something you don't want to do to create a new habit. You are conditioning your unconscious mind for 21 days allowing it to do it for you!

Conditioning Yourself for Success

Little Choices Create Big Outcomes

How do you spend your time? What do you focus upon? Are your choices moving you toward your desires or away from them? Can you imagine that in less than 15 minutes a day you can train your unconscious mind to work for you? As discussed above, your unconscious mind is responsible for all your body processes as well as all of your automatic responses (like quickly pulling your hand back from a hot stove). Your unconscious mind is also responsible for all of your emotions!

Furthermore, your unconscious mind never sleeps. While your conscious mind takes a break for six to eight hours every night, your unconscious mind keeps working. It dreams your dreams, resolves emotions and events that happened during the day, assimilates the learnings of the day, and so on. It also coordinates the autonomic processes in your body, keeping your heart pumping and your lungs breathing all night long.

Alpha Brain Waves

It has been shown that your conscious mind doesn't fully wake up right when your feet hit the floor in the morning. The reverse is true before you go to bed, that your conscious mind starts drifting off to sleep before you actually fall asleep. Put another way, you are in a deeper brain wave pattern, called an "alpha" brain wave pattern, right after you wake up and just before you actually go to sleep. It's that time when you are feeling a little groggy. So what does this mean to you and how can you use this information?

Alpha brain wave patterns are a deeper level of brain wave activity that effectively bypass the filtering mechanisms of your conscious mind. Alpha brain waves allow whatever you are exposed to while in this state to get stored in your mind much more easily. It is a brain state of accelerated learning. As your unconscious mind filters nothing in this state and lets everything in, positive or negative, you can learn very rapidly.

For example, if you listen to the television as "background noise" just upon waking or just before going to bed, you are bypassing your conscious filter and putting that information directly into your mind, as if it were the "truth." Your conscious mind, the skeptical truth-sifting part of your brain, is not as aware and does not question the information coming in. The unconscious mind takes the positive and negative, fact and opinion, and stores it all as "truth." So if you are watching a news program and listening to war updates, you are programming yourself with the associated feelings of hurt, fear, sadness, violence, distrust, etc. If you do this everyday, the way you think about everything is changed.

Your mind is like a dog, you have to train it!
– Terry Cole-Whittaker, author, inspirational
speaker and previous executive producer and
star of an Emmy award winning six-year
international television program

Training Your Mind

What are you training your mind to think about? What are you training it to believe about you or your world? The key to using the power of your mind in this alpha state is simple. Expose yourself to the "world you desire" every night just before you go to sleep! That's it. It's that easy. For example, I keep a 3" x 5" note card on my nightstand with the five most important things I want to create in my life written on it, one in each of the five life categories I focus upon: financial, relational, intellectual, physical and spiritual. I hold this card, read it, and feel the feelings as if I have already achieved these things, before going to bed each evening. (I've now memorized it, so I can focus less on reading and more on feeling like it's already happening in my life!)

I make it as real as I can in my mind and hold that feeling for several minutes as I lay down in bed. Then just before I drift off to sleep I think of three things I am grateful for in my life. This is simple yet very powerful. This programs my mind to think about my desires and how to achieve them all night long since my unconscious mind is being positively programmed every night. Since it never sleeps, it begins to plan out the solutions to my desires while I'm asleep!

Also, since I'm in a positive state after focusing on and expressing gratitude in my life, I get to "feel good" just before going to bed. My unconscious mind then associates my desires (from my note card) with my sense of feeling good (from my gratitude focus) and works to bring me more (due to the Law of Attraction) of what makes me feel good!

Try it for yourself! Perhaps this sounds too simple or too easy. I love simple, easy, effortless solutions. Decide what you want in each area of your life, simply and clearly. Then program your unconscious mind every night. For an extra boost, do what I do and repeat this process as the very first thing each morning too. This really starts your day off right, by imagining all that I desire and feeling gratitude for a new day. It works. It's easy. I feel great every day I do it, and not so calm and centered on the days I don't. As you begin to create this new habit, you'll begin to notice your desires materializing in your world. This will really get you motivated as you see your desires coming true!

For example, as you start meeting people who can help you achieve your desires, you begin to create evidence of the Law of Attraction working in your life. As you begin having new ideas about various ways to materialize your desires, you create more evidence. As you more easily stick to your new empowering habits you feel better about yourself. You begin to trust the process. In short, your life starts feeling great even before getting everything you said that you wanted in your life!

Radical Actions

What else are you filling your conscious and unconscious minds with? I used to listen to the news – everyday! I'm not against the news, but how long do you need to listen to this information? Are you listening to get informed or are you getting inundated with the same information over and over again. When is the last time some fantastically positive event was reported? (Fantastic things do happen in our world everyday!) Is there truly balance in the news reporting? Have you ever wondered why they are so focused on negative news? Is this really an accurate view of the world? Do you really believe the world is populated with more bad people than good? Do you really believe that there is more bad news in the world than good? Think about it and what you are training your mind to believe.

A year ago, I took a radical action. I disconnected my cable television service. Since I receive no television reception within it, this action effectively disconnected all my television programming. Of course, I know that there are some positive shows on the air, but I realized that watching television had an overall weakening effect on me. Aside from all the time that I was spending each day, which may have been better spent, I realized that the focus on fear and violence in television programming has become so pervasive. I simply chose not to feed my mind any more of that negative "programming." Now I rent selected, uplifting, positive-themed movies to watch at home. I self-program, rather than allow the television networks (whether broadcast, cable or satellite networks) to program me.

Habits Either Strengthen You or Weaken You

Do your habits strengthen you or weaken you? You probably know which habits have what effect on you if you just listen to your intuition. When you are honest with yourself, you'll likely know whether watching a TV show, reading a magazine, belonging to a social group, or other habitual actions you take are supportive or not. Why choose those things that weaken you? Choose thoughts, words and actions that strengthen you!

You are the personal trainer for your own mind. Just as a personal fitness trainer helps train your body for physical strength, you train your mind everyday based on your mental training regimen. For example, do you watch the news on television for more than 20 minutes a day? If so, it's probably too much. Are you watching television just before going to bed. It's probably not a supportive choice. Are you spending quiet time with yourself, at least 20 minutes of reflection, meditation or prayer each day? If so, you are probably more clear and centered than most people. Trust your intuition to complement your rational mind. Are you listening to what it's telling you?

Every habit, indeed every action in life, either strengthens you or weakens you. Choose those that strengthen you and you become stronger, more resilient and more successful. Choosing otherwise undermines your power. As everything either strengthens or weakens you, choose your actions carefully. And remember, everything counts.

What Do You Believe?

Your True Beliefs

Let's look at your beliefs. Do you see yourself as powerful, resourceful and resilient or do you see yourself otherwise? What's the truth? Your beliefs started out simply as ideas or thoughts, oftentimes not even originally yours. You acquired all of your earliest beliefs from your parents, your community, your school, your church or other influential people while growing up. Many of your beliefs have been left unquestioned by you as an adult. Some of these beliefs may have even become your most powerful beliefs. By adulthood, these beliefs probably are supported by well-practiced behaviors, patterns of both thought and action. As you mature, however, many beliefs no longer serve you. They may have been useful as a child but adults don't require the same kinds of beliefs. Beliefs like, "Don't talk to strangers" (the belief that strangers may be dangerous), may not serve you any longer. For example, this belief would not serve you in the context of building community or conducting business.

Whether you think you can or
you can't, either way you're right.
– Henry Ford

What beliefs support you or hold you back? Do you believe in yourself and your ability to create the life you desire? You can choose beliefs that support and empower you. All beliefs start out simply as thoughts. Thoughts are then repeated and become a habitual way of thinking. These thinking habits become what we call beliefs. Once a belief is created, it is rarely questioned, and assumed to be true.

Byron Katie, author of *Loving What Is* writes, "Nothing you believe is true. To know this is freedom." With this in mind and knowing that all beliefs start out simply as thoughts, try this exercise in re-programming any beliefs you would like to change. First, write down 5 to 10 supportive thoughts that would make it easy, or easier, for you to accomplish your goals. Here are some ideas:

- The more things I try, the more I learn.
- The most successful people have learned by making the most mistakes.
- I am every bit as worthy and deserving as everyone else on this planet.
- I am worthy of love: to love and to be loved.
- Every mistake strengthens my resolve.
- The quicker I fail, the quicker I can try something else, and the sooner I'll become successful.

What other thoughts would you like? Add these too. Then read your list everyday. Look for evidence of your new beliefs. There is always evidence for any belief you choose. Start by noticing that you are the same as everyone else, with your own sets of strengths and weaknesses. If that's true, then you are as deserving as everyone else. As you are more like others than different, and as they are worthy of love, then clearly you are too. Use the power of your rational, conscious mind to prove, step by step, as I have just done that these beliefs are indeed as true as anything else you used to believe. Then rather than trying to remove the old beliefs, simply remove your focus from them and focus on your new empowering beliefs. In no time at all your new beliefs will start feeling more and more real to you and will supplant the old, out-of-date beliefs. Remember to use the power of the Law of Attraction by focusing only on the new, empowering beliefs. The old ones will then begin to fade away automatically.

How Are You Being?

Have you ever thought about how you were being in a certain situation? Were you being happy and joyful, angry and bitter, frustrated and powerless, or perhaps fearful and depressed? Did you know that just as you can habituate ways of doing, you can also habituate ways of being? In life, you get what you think about. What your mind focuses upon and its alignment, or misalignment, to what you want creates a corresponding emotion. This emotion is your state of "being". Empowering "being" habits such as choosing to be courageous, patient or caring, allow you to come into alignment with your true self. When you are in alignment, you experience emotions like joy, love, appreciation and freedom. Ultimately, powerful being habits, where you practice embodying the positive attributes you desire, can transform your life.

Furthermore, I believe that you can control your thoughts. I'm not suggesting that you have to or are even able to monitor every thought. You are not in 100% control of what you think moment to moment. What I am suggesting is that you can always do two things to varying degrees to shift the focus of your thoughts. First, you can direct your focus consciously to that which you want. For example, on a party cloudy day you may see it as partly cloudy, or you may see it as partly sunny. Now this is a very simple example, but the idea is to focus upon the same situation in a different way. You may focus on the homeless people in your community and how they have a difficult time living day to day or you can think about all the people that are helped by food shelters, soup kitchens, and community programs that exist to assist them. This is not to say that we shouldn't do more or that the situation is somehow acceptable as is. Rather, it's an example of how you can create different emotional states by choosing what you focus on. Shifting your focus is easy, quick and powerful.

Another thing you can do is to question your thought. You may find it difficult to focus your thoughts on the positive or on what you desire at all times, especially if you have habituated feelings such as overwhelm, helplessness and victimhood. Can you believe that many people really do unconsciously choose to create these emotional states, really wanting to feel them? It's true. There is so much power in habits that some people would rather feel poorly or uncomfortable because it's familiar rather than experience positive and empowering feelings because it may be too unfamiliar.

It's always the case that such people also experience some benefit in their negative states. For example, people who play the role of "victim" are used to getting attention. Well-meaning, supportive people tend to pity them and try to help. Some people are then conditioned to associate being a victim and having their needs for support and love met in this "negative" way. They condition this negative feeling into a habit due to the positive results that they receive. If you notice negative habits of being, choose a new focus. Focus on what is good in the situation. Be grateful for the power you have to direct your thoughts to something that feels better. (We'll discuss gratitude in more detail in a later chapter.)

You must first be who you really are,
then do what you need to do,
in order to have what you want.
– Margaret Young, an early 20th century
American singer

Questioning Your Beliefs

When you question your thoughts, you cause them to be scrutinized by your conscious mind. You bring the thought, supportive or unsupportive, into your awareness. Here are 4 easy questions that can powerfully diffuse thoughts that do not serve you. By the way, how do you know if you are having a thought that does not serve you? It's easy! Does it feel good, or not? Good-feeling thoughts are supportive; bad-feeling thoughts are not.

The following is another exercise in re-programming your beliefs. Taken from *The Work* by Byron Katie, it allows you to use the power of your conscious mind to question the validity of any non-supportive thoughts or beliefs. These non-supportive thoughts are referred to as bad-feeling thoughts in her work. Here's the process.

Regarding the bad-feeling thought, ask yourself:

1. Is it true?

    a. Close your eyes, be still, and listen to your intuition as you contemplate your answer.

    b. If your answer is no, continue to Question 3.

2. Can you absolutely know that it's true?

    a. Can you really know what's best for you in the long run?

   b. Can you absolutely know that you would be happier if you got what you wanted?

3. How do you react when you think that thought?

   a. How does it feel when you believe that thought?

   b. Does that thought bring peace or stress into your life?

   c. How do you treat yourself or others when you believe that thought?

   d. Can you find a peaceful reason to keep that thought?

4. Who would you be without the thought?

   a. Close your eyes and imagine your past without that thought.

   b. What are you without that thought?

   c. Who are you without "your story"? (That it, the story you have created regarding the bad-feeling thought, such as why you have that belief or how it came to you.)

If you are feeling some relief from these questions, I encourage you to learn more about this simple yet powerful approach by visiting thework.com or learning more about Byron Katie's teachings.

Strength in Flexibility

To be successful you must start from where you are today. You will never be in the perfect place with the perfect idea and the perfect solution. You will never get permission to do what you want in all areas of your life. You will never get approval ahead of time for what you desire. You must simply decide, believe in yourself, believe that you deserve it and then take the actions that move you forward toward your desires.

I couldn't wait for success,
so I went ahead without it.
–Jonathan Winters, an American comedian

Things rarely turn out exactly as we have planned. This shouldn't sound like a new idea, but it is common to see people get frustrated, get off track, or even give up when things don't go their way. There are many paths up the mountain to your desires. You must remain flexible enough to see other ways that may appear or other opportunities to accomplish the same thing you want but in ways that may be different from your original plan. As we mentioned previously, be flexible like a strong-rooted willow tree, a tree that handles high winds very well due to its flexible branches. Rather than snap under high winds like harder, more brittle trees, willows sway. You must be like a willow tree. Sway in the winds of life, yet remain rooted firmly in the ground. Take a stand, yet be open to new ideas, solutions or paths that lead up the mountain of your dreams.

Do not wait; the time will never be 'just right'.
Start where you stand, and work with whatever
tools you may have at your command, and
better tools will be found as you go along.
– Napoleon Hill, author of the 1937 landmark
book, "Think and Grow Rich"

You Are Different

In pursuing your dreams,you don't need to be like everyone else. The world already has one of each of them. The world needs someone just like you. Many people talk to me about leaving a legacy in the world after they're gone and doing something worthy of their efforts. In short, they want to make a difference. I often ask them, "What kind of difference do you think you can make if you do things the same way as everyone else?"

You have to be different to make a difference.
Otherwise you can only make a 'same-ness'!
– Marc Carignan

Be willing to step into your own truth, walk your own path, adopt your own mission, create your own vision, and take whatever actions you are inspired to take to reach your goals. Honor your own unique perspective and your own ways of doing things. Don't ignore the great ideas of others but pursue your own great ideas as well. The world is most beautiful when it represents the mosaic of great ideas, points of view and diversity that comes from those brave enough to step forward and be "different."

The Power of Focus

Your Intention-Attention Balance

James Ray, author of *The Science of Success*, uses the term "Intention-Attention Balance" to refer to the interplay between your intention (what you desire) and your attention (what you focus upon). You must practice to become adept at this balance where you bring your focus – your thoughts, feelings and actions – in alignment with your desires. James refers to this as "going three for three", where all three aspects of your intention-attention balance, that your thoughts, feelings and actions, are all "firing in the same direction," that is, they are aligned with the same intention.

What we focus on expands.
– Various

Remember, where you place your attention is a powerful choice you make in every moment. Our Universe is a vibrational universe. As such, it is an "inclusive" Universe meaning that you cannot "exclude" vibrations from the mix created by your attention. Whatever you bring into your focus and attention becomes part of this mix, a sort of vibrational soup. Whether you place your attention on something you want or something you don't, you are focusing your energy. Success comes when you give your attention to the positive, choosing for example to be financial abundant rather than debt-free. These ideas vibrate differently and will create dramatically different results in your life.

The Value of Planning

Effective planning is an important leadership skill. As your vision becomes bigger and more complex, using your conscious mind's ability to coordinate and organize ideas and information can add value to your actions, keeping you and groups of people you may lead all moving in the direction of your intention. It is important to realize that although planning is an important activity, it does not guarantee results. The more complex the plan, the more likely that parts of it will occur quite differently that what you had planned. This is not to say that the plan was in error. No amount of planning can ever accurately envision every possible outcome.

Most people spend more time planning a two-week vacation then they do planning their lives.
– Terry Cole-Whittaker

A key benefit of planning is to focus your mind on your most important activities. There are many techniques for prioritizing and communicating priorities. There are many different paper and electronic mechanisms as well. As I like simple, straightforward solutions, I will present my favorite, the Daily Priority Note Card.

The Daily Priority Note Card

The Daily Priority Note Card approach is about focusing your attention on your most important tasks. Despite having busy days, imagine what your days would be like if you only needed to focus on three things each day to move your entire life (or your business) in the direction you choose?

Do you currently manage your life or your business with big to-do lists, stacks of sticky notes, or piles of paper with notes scrawled on them that never seem to get done? Do you spend time worrying about getting your lists crossed off, juggling the items on your lists and carrying most of them over to another day? Do you envision someday getting to the bottom of your lists? Perhaps you have already given up on organizing and rather just try to remember what's most important and do those things each day, hoping you didn't forget anything urgent? I once heard someone say that when you die your inbox – and your to-do list – will still be full! No doubt. So what's the solution?

If you want to reduce stress and increase your effectiveness, don't try to juggle lots of things that rarely get completed. Rather, try this simple approach for a week and watch it increase your effectiveness and how you feel about getting things done. When you apply this technique to your life and your work, you'll likely have time remaining to do other items on your list as well. Plus my clients regularly tell me how much better they feel about using this simple technique, knowing they are getting the most important items for the day completed.

Using The Card

At the start of each day, take a blank 3" x 5" white note card (or small sheet of paper) and write "PRIORITIES" at the top followed on the next line by the date. Write only the top three activities that you choose for that day. It's important to select the three activities carefully, sufficiently breaking them down in order to make each item able to be completed in no more than about one to two hours each. Select each item based on its ability to move you towards your major goals. Also, write the three priorities in the order of importance, with the first item being the most important task for the day. Here's an example:

PRIORITIES

Monday, August 29th

1. Complete executive coaching report; email to client for review.

2. Modify contract terms for XYZ company; email.

3. Celebrate birthday with friends and family.

When you start your day, do your priority tasks first and do them in order. Cross them off as you complete them. Don't let email, phone calls or any of your less important tasks detract or interrupt you from completing these items. The tasks that you have written down on this card are those that are most important to achieving your goals (as determined by you), and ultimately most important in manifesting your vision. When the three tasks are done, write "VICTORY" across the card – and smile. The rest of the day is yours to use as you choose, such as handling all the smaller tasks that you want to attend to, or getting started on some new ideas, either personally or professionally. One of my clients shared with me that they select two business and one personal priority each day, moving them forward in their life, in business and personally. Of course, they now do even more than three things, but this card commits them to the three most important things for the day. Feel good about moving your top three actions forward! Then toss the card out triumphantly!

Commitment Conditions You for Success

The Power of Commitment

There is power in commitment. When you become committed, you tell your unconscious mind that you are determined to find a way to achieve the goals on the way to your desires. Commitment supports you when the inevitable problems or road blocks show up. Road blocks appear more like speed bumps along your journey, slowing you down perhaps but never stopping you completely. When you are committed, you are more likely to search for alternatives rather than limit your strategy to just one or two methods. You condition yourself to keep taking action long after others have given up. In short, commitment is an indispensable trait of leading by intention.

When your desires are strong enough
you will appear to possess superhuman
powers to achieve.
– Napoleon Hill

How Many Times Must I Fail?

The most successful people tend to fail the most. Probabilities say that the more times you try, the more times you will fail. With each failure, however, comes a lesson. Don't miss learning from the lessons. As you learn what doesn't work, you get closer to what does. The more you try and the more you persist, the better your chances of success. In many ways, life is a "numbers game." The more you risk, try or attempt something, the more likely that one or more of your strategies will work! If you keep trying, learning and persisting, there is nothing you cannot achieve.

Oh what the heck, go for it anyway!
– Jack Canfield mantra

My favorite anecdote about staying committed is a story about Thomas Edison, the inventor of the light bulb (and many other inventions). He was ridiculed at the time, as he was making mistake after mistake, over 10,000 to be exact. He had a singular vision of an incandescent light bulb, a glowing ember inside of a glass dome. He didn't know for sure the amount of energy to use, the filament materials that would work best, the gas that should be used to fill the globe, and so on. When asked, he would simply say that he had not yet found the solution, but know knew thousands of ways that would not work. Shortly after his 10,000th try, he built a sustainable model of the light bulb, an invention that revolutionized the world. He persisted in his vision, fueled by his commitment, until he succeeded. He seemed to have an inner "knowing" that he would succeed – and he did!

You may have a fresh start any moment you
choose, for this thing that we call 'failure' is not
the falling down, but the staying down.
– Mary Pickford, a 20th century Canadian
motion picture star

But This Feels Uncomfortable

Have you ever not acted because you were scared, or felt uncomfortable? Perhaps you didn't want to make a certain phone call, send an email, or write a letter? Have you ever avoided a social gathering because you felt uneasy or uncomfortable? I've noticed that although these feelings have sometimes come up for me in my life, that when I start doing something uncomfortable that I know will support me, I find a good reason to do it and find something I enjoy about it. This causes the discomfort to lessen within me. Sometimes it even subsides altogether. Who knows, in time it may even become comfortable or even fun.

Everything new and uncomfortable becomes
comfortable in time.
– Terry Cole-Whittaker

There are growth opportunities in every discomfort. We grow as humans only when we challenge our "comfort zone." When we take a risk and are willing to do something we don't feel totally ready or prepared for, we grow. We basically have two choices. We either shrink back, changing nothing, or we step forward in confidence, opening up new opportunities for growth. Ultimately, growth is the mechanism for us to experience greater levels of joy and freedom in our lives. (We'll discuss the topic of confidence shortly.)

Little things don't mean a lot.
Little things mean everything.
– James Malinchak, founder of
"College Speaking Success"

It's the Little Things

It isn't just the big things we do that make a difference in our lives or in the lives of others, it's the little things. It is writing handwritten notes to friends or to customers, it is the quiet time you take to be alone, it is about being the first to give credit to others for what they've done rather than seek credit, and it is treating other people as the uniquely magnificent beings they are. It's about doing the little things in your own life that ultimately change your own quality of life, such as eating healthy foods, exercising regularly, and taking time for rest and relaxation.

In life, little ideas can grow into huge opportunities. In fact, all big ideas started out as little ideas. Did you know that the internet, the way we send email to each other, browse web pages and now even make phone calls (using VOIP technology) started out as just an idea to share information in a connected "web" of academic researchers and the US government? That little idea has in our lifetimes transformed the world, opening up markets never before opened to us!

Find the Inspiration Within

Find Your Inner Leader

To truly be happy, you must learn to tap into your "inner guidance." I sometimes think of this as my "inner leader." What is this inner voice, or intuition within you, leading you towards? Many people get inspired by things around them all the time. For me, I enjoy walking in nature, listening to music or viewing art. Although these external influences can help me feel inspired, it is ultimately about connecting to something within me, even as I assimilate these outer experiences.

If you are really honest with yourself, life is not really about creating all the stuff you want in your life. I'm not saying that you should abandon your desires – far from it. But rather, find alignment, or a "resonance" within, that allows you to experience that what you are doing here on earth is worthy of you, important to you, and serves a purpose that you care about. Getting rich is excellent. Having health and fitness is great. Attracting supportive relationships is important too. It's all part of the equation.

In any event, get to know yourself better. Know thyself. Focus on your own "spiritual" growth, that reflection about who you truly are inside and find (or choose) your purpose for being here. For some of you this spiritual growth may include a focus on religion. For others, it will include learning about metaphysics, connecting to nature, or meditative practices. The journey is to recover your dreams and then envision the difference you can make in the lives of those you love and the world at large. This will lead you to your reason for being here, your purpose.

Follow effective action with quiet reflection.
From this quiet reflection will come even more
effective action.
– Peter F. Drucker, a 20th century writer and
management consultant; made the term
'knowledge worker' famous, ushering in the
'knowledge economy'

Trust Your Intuition

Have you ever had an "ah-ha" moment where you had a spark of insight about what life was really about, or perhaps felt that you were in the "flow" for even just a moment? This is an indication of being on the path of your spiritual development, or your journey of enlightenment. It is tapping into that deeper truth within you, beyond simply your mind and body. It is connecting to that place within, a place of inspiration, a place without form, a place that we can call "spirit." (Note that this definition is not limited to any specific religious traditions but rather intended as the description of a Universal concept.)

This place of Spirit is the place from which creativity originates. In his book, *The Seven Spiritual Laws of Success*, Deepak Chopra refers to Spirit as a place of "pure potentiality." Remember that your mind is more like a radio receiver than that which actually authors the thoughts. This is not to diminish anything that you may think about. It's simply that when you are vibrating at a certain level, you automatically begin to receive thoughts and ideas that are "in tune" with that vibration (like tuning into a radio station). In fact, everything that exists in physical form (hence the term "in-form-ation") was at one time just a thought, formless and non-physical (what we call "in-spir-ation"). Learning to master the connection to your Spirit, or inspiration, is a key to "tuning into" your joy and happiness.

Create an Evidence Journal

Let me suggest a final exercise in this chapter. Create an "evidence journal." Before going to bed each night, using a small notepad and pen that you can keep by your bedside, briefly write three items. Each item you write down should be a separate example of evidence, however small, of how your desires are manifesting or beginning to manifest in your life. This might be an introduction to someone new, an idea for a new product or service you could offer, or an insight into a different path to your goal. It might be that you simply felt lighter, more calm, and less stressed about the process of pursuing your goal. Whatever the evidence, write it down.

This process will begin to convince you (and particularly your conscious mind), day by day, of the progress that you're making. Watching things manifest is a great part of this whole process. Sure, getting all the stuff you want is good too, but who you become and what you attract along the way makes the whole trip worthwhile.

LEADERSHIP

INTENTION

VISION

PRACTICE

CONFIDENCE

ATTITUDE

LEARNING

Chapter 5. Confidence is Believing the Truth About You

Who Are You, Really?

When you base your confidence on who
you are instead of what you can accomplish,
you have created something that no one or no
circumstance can ever take away from you.
– Barbara De Angelis, best-selling author,
television personality and motivational speaker

Beyond Titles and Roles

Who are you? Beyond the titles you hold and the roles you play, who are you really? I know that you may be a mother or father, a brother or sister, an employee, an employer or even retired. You hold a Ph.D., an M.D., a college degree, or have pursued or completed some other program. These are all part of who you are, yet they are not really you.

Many people base their confidence on what they've done or what they know. Some people become confident because of who they know. These choices all presuppose the same thing. They assume that your confidence, your self-perceived value or importance as a person, is due to what you've done, who you've met or what you know. It is tied to things that have occurred outside of you. As valuable as those things are to you in the world, they also are not the real you.

What Confidence Is Not

So if it isn't these things that gives you confidence, what does? On a similar note, what takes away your confidence? It seems like most people I meet want more confidence. Many seem to be waiting for confidence to come to them. They are waiting for something to occur to become more confident. They are waiting to lose weight, or earn their degree, or succeed in business. Are you waiting to do something that's important to you until you get the confidence? Have you been waiting for a while?

Some people think that confidence is "believing in your ability to do certain things." People look at their ability to be good at their job, good at the dating scene, good in love and romance, good at making money, and so on. This type of confidence can be very supportive in doing the things you already do well, but what about the things that you have not yet mastered? The limitation about thinking about confidence in this way is that if you don't know how to do something well, you are not likely to be confident.

There are only so many skills and abilities that you can learn and master in your lifetime. There's only so much time. True confidence goes beyond believing in your ability to be consistently successful at the things that you've already mastered. After all, if confidence was just based on doing things well, there would be a lot more confident people in the world. Each one of us does at least a few things well, yet so few people are truly confident in the world.

To clarify this point, ask yourself the following questions. What have you accomplished in the world regarding your job titles? What about your life roles, such as parent, sibling, etc? What jobs have you held successfully? What experiences have caused you to be proficient at certain skills? What abilities have you learned competently or even masterfully? Now ask yourself, are you confident in each and every one of those areas?

For most people, despite all this evidence, they still are not confident. They may be confident about one thing or another, but they are not confident about themselves. So perhaps confidence really isn't about knowing how to do something or having done a thing well in the past. If it was, you would have felt great after putting in all that effort and achieving your successes. In fact, you would still be feeling confident about it today!

Confidence isn't really about achieving all those things: the titles, the roles, the degrees or the recognitions. Each of these things indicate various accomplishments, but they do not guarantee your confidence. So what is confidence?

What Confidence Is

According to Barbara De Angelis, "True confidence is believing in your ability to do and act regardless of the situation." It is believing in your will and your resolve as a person to do whatever is required. It is a belief in yourself as beyond your physical body and its limitations. It's a belief in your spirit, the "human spirit." It's knowing that no matter what challenges are presented in your life, you will have the strength to take action and handle it.

Confidence is a willingness to act. It's a belief in yourself as a person, worthy of good things and positive results in the world. It's believing that you will act and you will accomplish what you want in your life. It's less about your ability, your skills or your talents, and more about your ability to take action.

How often do you talk yourself out of your success? Is it just a fluke when good things happen for you? You don't have to be perfect to be confident. You don't have to have all the answers. You don't even need to know the whole solution before you start.

Genius doesn't mean knowing everything;
it means knowing where to find whatever
you need to know.
– Terry Cole-Whittaker

How Confidence Works

Confidence means that if you decide you're going to do something, you know that you can start from wherever you are and learn whatever you need to learn to get to your goal. You don't have to be the best to start, you simply have to believe in your ability to learn along the way.

Writing this book for me has required much confidence. I had never written a book. I did not know all the things I would need to learn in writing it, editing it, publishing it, marketing it and so on. Yet, I decided to write it. I realized that I could learn what I needed to learn along the way. People showed up in my life to assist me, people who had previously written and published books. Clients and friends offered to proofread and comment on early drafts of the book. Each person who contributed added a new perspective and depth to the book. I ultimately got to make choices within the book among the various perspectives and among my various experiences, giving me a larger set of options from which to choose.

I kept walking down the path, tripping every now and then, learning what I needed to learn as I went along. I learned a lot about how I structure information in my mind, and how to use tools such as outlines and quotes that I had been accumulating for many years to enhance the book. After my first draft, I began seeing more clearly the flow of the book, which started out as only a high-level outline. After my first draft, I gained much more clarity about how to connect the individual chapters into a cohesive whole. This would not have happened if I had not begun the book, stepped into this unknown process, and began "walking the path" of writing the book. I also know that as good as I intend this book to be, that as I continue to write subsequent books, each will get better and better. In short, I tapped into the confidence within myself. I believed in my ability to take the actions necessary to be successful. And so can you.

Trusting in Yourself

Trying Until You Succeed

Confidence does not mean you will never make mistakes. Far from it! It means that when you make mistakes, you accept them as learning opportunities in your life. Much as Edison saw his mistakes as learning experiences, you too can choose to look at your mistakes and failures as opportunities to learn. I've learned after many years of studying peak performance and personal development that the most successful people make the most mistakes. To truly be successful requires taking risks that most people are unwilling to take. To become very successful requires that you try out a lot of things, many of which will not work out. Success is continuing to try things until you find what works. You are looking for the 10,000th try when the light bulb solution appears. For most of us, our goals will likely require far less than 10,000 tries in order to achieve success.

Another thing to remember is that you can't make that make mistakes over and over again without learning something. Edison knew this too. Look for the lessons in each mistake and realize that each mistake brings you closer to success. After all, you now know another way that does not work. The only mistake is not learning from these failed approaches.

Ultimately, you must believe in your internal resolve, in your "will." You can learn whatever skills you need. You can learn from others' experiences along the way, but you must have the determination to do whatever you need to do. Stay persistent.

Don't Wait, Start Today

In some areas of my life, I used to believe that I had to master the skill or technique before I even began doing it. For example, when I first started supporting people with life coaching, I was nervous. I felt like I wasn't fully prepared. I was concerned about not knowing how to handle every possible circumstance that may arise. I did, however, move forward in confidence with a clear intention of being in service to my clients, learning what I needed to along the way. (I had already been trained, yet did not have the experience that one gains from many hours of coaching.)

If I had never started coaching other people I would never have learned from so many wonderful clients. I would have missed the opportunity to support so many people. Of course, my early sessions weren't as smooth and polished as they are now, but just like when I learned to ride a bicycle, I skinned my knee and fell down a few times on my road to mastery. If I don't fall down occasionally, I'm probably not taking big enough risks to truly be successful! I wonder how different my life would have been if I would have given up learning to ride a bike the first time I fell off.

There is no need to wait. You will never do something masterfully the first time you do it. You did not ride a bike perfectly the first time. You weren't a great driver the first time you got behind the wheel. And you won't be an expert the first time you try anything else that is new to you. If you are waiting to learn everything you need to know before you start, I say, "Get over it!"

You must start where you are today. You must have "initiative." The word, initiative, is based on the word initiate, or "to start." So start where you are. Only then can "persistence," the key to maintaining your success, take over. There's nothing to persist about, however, unless you get started. One thing I learned about initiative is this: It won't be any easier to start tomorrow than it will be to start today.

Do It Again and Again

You will never master something without doing it over and over again. As the old adage goes, "Repetition is the mother of skill." You must be willing to do whatever you want to master before you have actually mastered it. It is an integral part of the process to mastery. Children seem much more willing to try something new than adults are. Adults often seem to be hindered by a need to do something perfectly the first time.

A great example of this is in learning languages. Adults are said to learn languages much slower than children. It is said that when children learn languages, especially before the age of 7, they can speak each language fluently for life. Why is this? Are children's brains bigger? I realize that scientists point to increased activity in the brains of children. What if this is not the only reason? I propose that children are not held back by the fear of making mistakes when they are young – unless adults impose that fear upon them. When adults are in a safe, supportive environment, they too can rapidly learn a new language quickly and easily. (We'll discuss this further in the chapter on learning.)

Be willing to look silly. Be willing to get embarrassed. Be willing to trip and fall. Is it really such a high price to pay for mastery? Isn't it worth the achievement of your success? Confidence can support you in taking risks when that confidence is based internally, on the belief in your ability to take action. As the expression goes, you must be willing to get back up on the horse that bucks you.

Staying home waiting for confidence doesn't work either. If you're not sure what to do, simply start where you are. It's like learning to paddle a boat down the river. You don't need to wait for the perfect time, as there isn't one. You don't need to wait for the best weather or the smoothest current. Just put your boat in, jump aboard, and start paddling. Your first strokes may feel awkward and uncontrolled or you may wonder how to navigate the rocks that are popping up as you ride down river. You may need to learn how to manage the speed and intensity of the current, but you will learn. You may get some clues waiting on shore, but until you get in the water you cannot master it. Remember, it doesn't really matter where in the river you launch your boat. Wherever in the river you put in your boat, you can be sure that the current will carry it down river.

Take the first steps toward what you truly desire. The longer you wait the harder it will be for you to start. Don't talk yourself out of what you truly want. Don't beat yourself up for not starting earlier. That time has passed. All you have, and all you ever need, is right now. Don't wait, as this feeds the seeds of regret. Waiting also lessens your confidence in all areas of your life. Act now, act firmly and believe in your own internal confidence, your ability to do what it takes and to learn what you need to learn along the way. That's all the confidence you'll need to keep going and become truly successful!

Believe in yourself. Make mistakes. Learn along the way. Keep trying. Confidence will get you there. Remember that many people may have already achieved what you desire, or something quite similar. What are you willing to risk to get what you want? Don't you deserve it?

The Confidence is Within You Now

All I need is within me now!
– Anthony Robbins mantra

Belief and Trust

Believe in what you are doing. Believe you can endure. Believe you have the persistence to keep learning when everyone else stops. Believe in yourself as a person, not simply in your abilities. Your abilities can change as you keep learning. If you really desire it you can learn to invest well, become a successful entrepreneur, master a new profession and so on. Remember, your abilities are not the source of your confidence. The source lies within you, by believing in yourself.

Next, trust yourself. To do this you must keep promises to yourself. Do you commit to yourself and then let it go because, after all, it's "just a commitment to you?" Stop that. The most important commitments are self-commitments. When you break commitments to yourself, you erode your self-respect. Self-respect is an important aspect of trusting yourself. Trusting yourself is the true "heart" of confidence.

Be honest with yourself. Hold yourself up as an honorable and worthy person. Know that in keeping promises to yourself you become more empowered and confident in pursuing all of your endeavors. As you become more confident, more self-honoring and more self-respecting, people around you also benefit.

Somehow I can't believe that there are any heights that can't be scaled by a man who knows the secrets of making dreams come true. This special secret – curiosity, confidence, courage, and constancy – and the greatest of all is confidence. When you believe in a thing, believe in it all the way, implicitly and unquestionably.
– Walt Disney

The road to greatness is not crowded. The further you walk, the more elbow room there is for you to stretch out along the way and take in the scenery. Sometimes this road requires nimble dexterity, sometimes it requires power and strength to climb large boulders and at other times, it requires a machete to cut your way through rarely traversed forests. In any event, know that your efforts, fueled by your confidence, will set you apart in ways that will create new opportunities and new joys to be found.

Have the Courage

What is courage and how does it relate to confidence? I view it this way. Courage, taken from "coeur", the French word for heart, means to act "with heart." Courage, as applied to confidence, is taking action with love and sensitivity for yourself and others. It is choosing a path that is true to who you really are, close to your heart and meaningful to you. It is respecting others along your path. It is staying true to your life's purpose. It's about remembering that we are all connected. It's believing that others do not have to lose for you to win in life.

When "heart" is applied there is an emotional connection to success and confidence that cannot be duplicated by action alone. It goes deeper than simply manifesting your desires. When action and heart combine, you tap into "inspired action." It is inspired action that brings you into the "flow" of life, where intuition (connected to heart) and your actions seem to come easily and effortlessly. Things come together in ways that you may have not previously imagined. It brings joy, peace and love into your life. It is tapping into Universal Energy and connecting to the truth of who you truly are, a vibrational being connected to all that is. It is in this connection that all successes flow to you without resistance. It is the natural state of things.

The Road Less Traveled

True leaders require a higher level of confidence and courage than most people, as they must go to places that others have not gone, or even places that others have been unwilling to go. Leaders walk the road less traveled. Leaders tap into the power within, an energy that drives them forward. Intentional leaders inspire others to follow versus trying to control others by force. Leaders choose "power" over force, enrolling others in their vision rather than commanding them to obey. Are you such a leader?

In summary, confidence is not about what you know, but in your ability to act regardless of circumstances. It's a belief in your will as a person to be able to do whatever you choose. It's aligning yourself with the vision within and focusing upon your intention. Ultimately, confidence is believing in your ability to take whatever action in life that will be necessary to create all you desire.

LEADERSHIP

INTENTION

VISION

PRACTICE

CONFIDENCE

ATTITUDE

LEARNING

Chapter 6. Attitude Determines the Greatness of Your Life

It's Not What You Say, It's How You Say It

The Universe, God, whatever you choose to call it, only supports you in your greatness. It's not going to support you when you lessen yourself. It doesn't support you when you're dimming your own light, because it gave the light to you.
– Oprah Winfrey

What My Mom Taught Me

I remember as a child my Mother teaching me about communication. This was especially true in how I communicated with my brother and sister, both younger than I was. She would say, "It's not what you say, it's how you say it." I've thought a lot about that growing up, about how my words alone were not enough. She seemed to be telling me that my attitude (as exhibited by my body language or vocal tone) was inconsistent with my words. I was sometimes communicating something different than the words I was using, usually when I was upset or arguing with my siblings. I think she was right.

It's true that you can say just about anything if you know how to say it. "How" to say it refers to the non-verbal part of your communication and it's strongly connected to your attitude. A "positive attitude" creates a more welcoming tone in communication, but what do we really mean when we speak of having a positive attitude?

Sometime it's easier to look at a contrast. For example, we seem to know right away when someone has a "bad attitude." We know it when we see it or hear it. We might think of someone as being rude, impatient, inconsiderate, ungrateful, or even mean. So what is it to have a positive attitude? Well, using a more positive tone of voice, holding a calm body posture and using kind and respectful words would be considered positive. But how do we do that, especially when we don't "feel" like doing it?

You Are the Master of Your Emotions

Attitude is everything. Without a positive
attitude, all successes are hollow and
all mistakes are failures.
– Marc Carignan

The Emotional State Triad

Our thoughts are primarily responsible for the emotions we experience. Simply put, if you feel happy you are thinking happy thoughts. If you feel sad, you are thinking sad thoughts. As discussed earlier, your emotions work as a guidance system letting you know what you are thinking without having to self-monitor each and every thought.

How many times have you felt like your emotions were driving you? Have you ever felt like your feelings had a mind of their own, creating for you either a good day or a bad day? Are you ready to get in the driver's seat of your emotions? Well, you can! You can change your emotional state anytime you choose. You can choose a positive attitude anytime. It takes only a moment!

First, imagine a triangle with equal length sides, with a flat side down and a point facing up. Let's call this the Emotional State Triad. This triad, or triangle, has three sides, each representing one of the three options available for you to change your state.

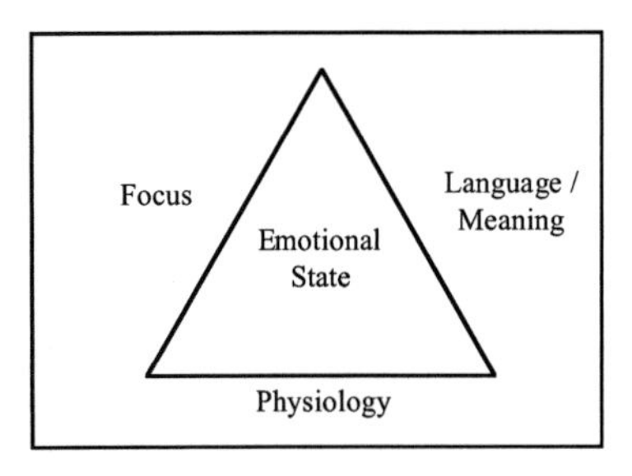

Let's start with the easiest and most powerful, represented by the bottom line of the triad. Label it "Physiology." Physiology refers to your body, particularly how you move and hold your body. Are you moving slowly and lethargically, or are you moving briskly with a bounce in your step? Are you holding your body slouched over or are you standing with your head high, shoulders back, and chest out? Changing your body's movement and posture affects how you feel instantly! The next time you feel tired stand up and cheer for 10 seconds. Or start smiling like a "crazy person" for 10 seconds. Start laughing out loud for no particular reason. Your emotional state will change, and quickly! But there's more you can do.

Next, look at the left side of the triad. Label it "Focus." Focus is what you think about. Are you focused on reasons why your life, your business, or your specific project might fail? Are you worried about money, or security, or loss? If you change your focus to something you want, you will change your state. If you think about what you're happy or grateful about in your life, you will change your state. Focusing on what's going well instead of what's not changes your emotions. It's not about pretending to feel better, but really focusing on something that's true and positive where you can direct your mind's focus.

Finally, look at the right side of the triad. Label it "Language / Meaning." The first part of this concept is language. The words you use in communicating matter. What words do you use to communicate to other people? What words do you use in your self-talk? Are you positive and supportive of yourself and others in your language?

Mind is the brain in action.
Mind is what the brain does.
– Joe Dispenza, biochemist, researcher of neurology, neurophysiology, and brain function; star of the movie, "What the Bleep Do We Know?"

Your Powerful Self-Talk

Regarding self-talk, when things aren't going your way do you tell yourself, "Here I go again. I'll never be able to do it." Or are you saying, "Oops, I guess that didn't work. I guess I'll just need to try something else!" Same event, different responses. Treat yourself with care, honor and respect and watch your emotional state change. How would you treat your best friend? Don't you deserve at least the same treatment when dealing with yourself? When you treat yourself with respect and use supportive language in your self-talk, you indirectly train others how to treat you. People pick up on these signals all the time.

What about the "how you say it" part? Beyond the words you use, what is your tone of voice? Are you coming across as irritated, honest, compassionate, loving, or something else? Your tone always communicates more than the actual words you use.

The second part, meaning, refers to the words you choose. Everyone has their own experience with and unique definition for specific words. You may use the same words as someone else but have a different interpretation. Even common words like love, fun and enthusiasm can have very different interpretations. The more you know someone, the more adept you can be in selecting words with the meanings that most match your desired communication. After all, the point of communication is in getting other people to understand what you mean, isn't it?

Anthony "Tony" Robbins, the well-known motivational speaker and master life coach, has been teaching this particular method for several decades. It has stood the test of time and millions of people around the world have practiced this simple solution to manage their emotional states easily and quickly. It has worked for them. It's likely to work for you too.

Fake It 'Til You Make It

You may have heard of the term "emotional intelligence." As opposed to IQ, referring to the Intellectual Quotient of an individual, emotional intelligence refers to being emotionally appropriate, flexible and mature. This is an increasingly important and popular topic in the workplace, especially when assembling people from various backgrounds, cultures and experiences. Such multi-cultural team members are challenged by communication differences, even though they may realize the benefits of diverse experiences and backgrounds among their team.

When you learn to manage your emotional states effectively, you become a more powerful communicator and contributor. Choosing to use the techniques of changing your physiology, your focus, and your language and its meaning takes a little practice. Even if this does not feel comfortable at first, just think, "Fake it 'til you make it". This doesn't mean that you should lie, but rather just "try on" a new emotion. Do this by changing your physiology, your focus or your language and meaning. Or do all three!

Simply use the emotional state triad techniques and watch your emotions shift from inappropriate to appropriate, from negative to positive. Don't let negative emotions limit your opportunities. Use these simple and powerful techniques.

PERSISTENCE TRUMPS EVERYTHING

You don't have to slow down, just calm down.
– Bob Proctor, motivational speaker, author and teacher; star of the movie, "The Secret"

PERSISTENCE BEATS KNOWLEDGE

Persistence is more powerful than knowledge, experience or expertise. This trait has created more millionaires and supported more people than perhaps any other talent, skill or mindset. Once you've put your plan into action, persistence keeps you going. It says that no matter what, you keep walking the path. You "keep on keeping on." You continue on good days and bad, when you feel like it and when you don't, and when you are tired and when you are well rested.

Persistence conditions your mind and your body for success. It creates a consistency of thinking and acting. It allows you to stay fully engaged in the game of life. It supports you in continuing to learn from what's working in your life, and what's not.

If you are persistent, you tend to keep involved and to keep at it, improving as you go along. For me, I choose to keep practicing because I want to "win" again tomorrow, and even bigger! I don't want to "rest on my laurels." Of course, I want to enjoy my successes along the way, to "smell the roses." Yet, I want to keep moving towards my ultimate desires. I want to make a bigger difference in my life and the lives of those I love. I want to make the positive difference I've dreamed of making in the world.

It's not about your IQ. It's about your 'I will.'
– James Malinchak

Persistence isn't about what you know, or how many times you've done something before. It's about resolve and it's about choice. It's deciding that you will continue to play the game of life even when it seems you may not be doing that well, or when you don't feel like doing it again today. It's about saying to yourself and others, "I will."

Be consistently persistent in the things most important to you. If you do, anything you desire can be yours. Your success is surely guaranteed. While people are dropping out or giving up, stay in the game. While others are saying enough is enough, keep playing. And when you think you can't go any further, take just one more step. As James Malinchak says, "It's not about your IQ. It's about your 'I will.'"

Choose Enthusiasm in Your Life

The definition of success is going from failure to failure without losing your enthusiasm.
– Winston Churchill

Be Enthusiastic

What is enthusiasm? Based on the Greek word, "enthousiasmos," it originally meant inspiration or "possession by the presence of a god." Today it typically means intense enjoyment, interest or approval. Being enthusiastic is a powerful motivator. It affects all areas of the emotional state triad. When you are enthusiastic, your physiology shifts to more dramatic and deliberate body motions, your focus lands on something positive and uplifting, and your language is supportive and excited.

It's interesting to see how closely this resembles many people's view of joy and happiness, and their definition of how success ought to feel. Enthusiasm, you see, is a choice. It is about picking a strategy of optimism, of constantly learning and of staying positive. It's about remembering that the bigger your dreams, the bigger your obstacles will be. Bigger obstacles bring more unknowns and more opportunities to fail along the way. Yet bigger dreams also bring the possibilities of greater growth, greater happiness and greater payoffs in life.

Ultimately, I believe that your success is far more than getting what you want. Your success is in how you choose to live your life. Your success is the way you approach your challenges and your activities day to day. It's about how you treat yourself and others. It's about your world view and how you see yourself in it. It is keeping your enthusiasm, your passionate interests and your eagerness to continue on towards the greater goal. All of this is true success.

Gratitude is a Magnet for Positive Experiences

Whatever we think about and
thank about we bring about.
– John Demartini

Gratitude is a Vibrational Strategy

Gratitude is energy, and energy vibrates. When you are grateful, you send out powerful vibrations that the Law of Attraction must return back to you. According to the Emotional Guidance Scale described earlier, gratitude (listed as "appreciation" on the scale) is on the top wrung of the ladder. It vibrates at the highest level of the emotional scale. Gratitude is a powerful force of attraction that feels good and brings even more to feel good about into your life. Feeling gratitude is as easy as focusing on the things in your life that you are already grateful for or appreciative of. We all have many things to be thankful for. This gratitude exercise is simply about bringing these things into focus.

Without gratitude, the perception of scarcity comes in our thinking. Scarcity describes a world where there isn't enough for everyone. It presumes that for you to have what you want, someone else cannot. It proposes that you must compete for the good stuff before someone else gets it.

It takes gratitude to eradicate this kind of thinking from your mind. We don't all have to compete for limited resources because the resources in the world are abundant. When people focus on scarcity, it leads them to greed, to competition and to a sense of lack. Lack then creates a sense of fear, of needing to hold on, and of thinking you need even more in case you "run out" of it later.

The reality is that there really is enough for everyone. There is abundance in the world. There truly is enough for you, for me and for everyone else. According to Wallace Wattles, in *The Science of Getting Rich*, "If your gratitude is strong and constant, the response you will receive will be strong and continuous. The movement of the things you choose will move toward you. You cannot exercise much power without gratitude because it is gratitude that keeps you connected with power."

Being Satisfied with Where You Are

There is a belief held by some people that you must be dissatisfied in order to be motivated to achieve something greater. This is something that I believed for some time as well. I no longer believe this. In fact, being continually dissatisfied with the way things are tends to attract more of what you don't want, creating ongoing frustration and disappointment.

Wattles writes, "The value of gratitude does not consist solely in getting more blessings in the future. Without gratitude you cannot keep from being dissatisfied with things as they are." I've certainly noticed this in my own life, especially during periods where I was not focused upon how grateful I was for everything that was going so well in my life. Even if it was the basics like having safe water to drink, healthy food to eat and a safe place to sleep tonight. Think of how many people in the world cannot even say those things today!

Gratitude Leads to Greatness

Wattles continues, "The moment you permit your mind to dwell with dissatisfaction upon things as they are, you begin to lose ground. You fix attention upon the common, the poor, the squalid, and the mean – and your mind takes the form of these things. You will then transmit forms or mental images to the formless. Thus, the common, the poor, the squalid, and the mean will come to you."

The "formless" Wattles talks about is that place of pure energy, where thoughts create. It is the Law of Attraction working to bring into your life what you are focusing upon. It is like an idea that a inventor has long before his machine is built or the vision a sculptor has while peering into a block of marble. It is like a desire that you choose to make a reality.

"To permit your mind to dwell upon the inferior is to become inferior and to surround yourself with inferior things. On the other hand, to fix you attention on the best is to surround yourself with the best and to become the best," Wattles says.

Choose to come from a place of gratitude. If you need to get clearer, write down several things you are grateful for in this moment. You might say that you are grateful for the eyes to read this book or the ears to hear it read (if you have the audio version, that is). You could add that you are grateful that you are healthy and are likely to eat nutritious, healthy meals today. You can consider the people you love and who love you, the opportunities that abound in your life and the wonderful skills and talents that you possess.

If you look around, there is plenty you can be grateful for. From this place of gratitude, look ahead to what's next. From this place of appreciation for "what is," then intend what's next for you. Whatever you do in life, do it in gratitude. Live your life with an "attitude of gratitude."

Leadership
Intention
Vision
Practice
Confidence
Attitude

Learning

Chapter 7. Learning is the Key to Mastery

Mastery is a Journey

Live as if you were to die tomorrow.
Learn as if you were to live forever.
– Mohandas "Mahatma" Gandhi

Don't Get Old

I believe we don't "grow" old. We simply "get old" when we decide to stop learning. Many people stop learning when they get a certain job, when they retire, or when they get to a certain age. Why? Did they lose their passion for learning something new?

Learning can and should be fun. There's always something to learn. First, you need to pick something you want to learn about, whether it's learning a language, improving your golf game or playing a musical instrument. Learning is a lifelong activity and a part of every leader's work. Whatever you choose, put your heart into it. Become passionate about it. Continue to pursue it, or something equally interesting to you, until you die.

I'm gonna live 'til I die! I'm gonna laugh 'stead of cry, I'm gonna take the town and turn it upside down, I'm gonna live, live, live until I die... Before my number's up, I'm gonna fill my cup, I'm gonna live, live, live, until I die!
– Frank Sinatra, as sung in
"I'm Gonna Live 'Til I Die"

Become masterful at the things that you are most attracted to learn. As you master these things, you will recognize that there is always more to learn. For me, I've found that to be true that in every part of life. The more I learn about a subject, the more I see there is to learn about it.

Become an Inspired Learner

The Standards of Presence

In 2003, a non-profit foundation created by Peter J. Reding and Marcia Collins was incorporated as the Foundation for Inspired Learning. This organization was created to take a body of work created by these two master facilitators and share it with the world. The Foundation's mission is to evoke the innate love of learning in each person and with each learning experience for a lifetime of "inspired learning."

The Inspired Learning Model™ accelerates learning and honors the innate learning process that each of us utilizes when we are at our most receptive. Utilizing the knowledge of how children naturally learn and applying those aspects that are often missing in both adult and child learning environments, a set of learning standards, the "Standards of Presence," was created and incorporated as one of the seven elements of the Model.

The underlying principle of these Standards is acceptance. In a group setting, there is an understanding and belief that everyone is doing their best to learn, grow, respect, and follow these Standards. Each "inspired learner" agrees to adhere to these standards to the best of their ability for the benefit of everyone's learning, including their own. Furthermore, self-acceptance is particularly beneficial in experiencing a safe, empowering environment to learn, create, communicate, and celebrate learning successes.

The Standards of Presence follow. When spoken by the inspired learners, each of the 10 standards is prefaced by, "It is my intention to ...":

1. Maintain confidentiality.

2. Adopt a stand for innocence.

3. Practice a positive focus.

4. Connect at a deep level.

5. Claim my experience as my own.

6. Listen deeply and with honor.

7. Give only authentic and positive acknowledgment and support.

8. Fully receive acknowledgment and support.

9. Practice self-care and self-responsibility, and allow others to do the same.

10. Be fully present.

Each of these intentions contributes to creating a powerful and unique learning environment, where it is safe and fun to explore and learn. It is OK to make mistakes in this environment, as well as to look silly or to stumble. It is an environment that focuses on "what is working" in the learning process rather than what's not. With the support of trained Inspired Learning Facilitators™ encouraging the learners, called "inspired learners," this environment is maintained through those periods when most learners, especially adult learners, would begin to "retreat" from the work of learning.

This retreat usually follows feelings of embarrassment, being unsure or not knowing how to proceed when the material being learned feels too unfamiliar. In this special learning environment, all feelings are welcomed and supported. Learners are not made to feel wrong or inadequate. Each sign of learning is acknowledged along the way, creating a growing momentum of learning and success. Any mistakes made or concerns held by inspired learners in this space are respected and allowed to be set aside, allowing them to lose intensity and melt away. As learners continue to learn in the Inspired Learning Environment™, they begin to pick up speed and make incredible leaps in the pace of learning in a fraction of the time that is required for people to learn in a traditional teaching environment. Beyond speed, there is a deeper level of learning that occurs, allowing the learner to relate to the information more powerfully than in other environments.

Looking More Deeply

Let's look at a few of the standards. Standard number two is, "It is my intention to adopt a stand for innocence." As a child would approach a new activity for the first time, inspired learners are invited to look at the activity, or what is being learned, in a new way. As adults, we often go into situations thinking, "Been there, done that." Not having to learn everything anew every time helps you operate more efficiently in your world, but it does not create the most powerful learning environment.

This standard encourages leaving all the thoughts of knowing how to do something "outside the room." This frees up each learner to make their own discoveries along the way, including the person who may have already learned something very similar. It is amazing how many new learnings, or distinctions, can be made when you free yourself from how you think an activity ought to look, or how it ought to work.

When you approach a learning opportunity in this way, you create space for yourself and others to try out new approaches and new ways of doing things. You get to release judgment and comparison and allow yourself, and others, to experiment. You allow yourself to "try on" a new approach or consider a new solution. Inspiration and creativity abound when this standard is practiced fully and authentically.

Standard number three is, "It is my intention to practice a positive focus." Look for the good in what's going on. Look for what's working. This standard, coupled with standard number seven, to "give only authentic and positive acknowledgment and support," is an extremely powerful combination. A big difference in the Inspired Learning Environment, which is being communicated here in these standards, is that it encourages the facilitators to deliberately ignore what's not working in the learning process by any of the learners. Yes, ignore it!

You might think, "How can things improve if I don't address the problems?" This is, of course, a reasonable question from the standpoint of traditional learning environments. The truth is that pointing out what people are doing "wrong" never works long term. In the short term, there may be an opportunity to correct a problem but the learner loses confidence. The learner loses the sense of joy in learning. Eventually, the learner stops engaging in any learning that may seem too risky, too different, or in an area where they may not succeed. These learners, whether in school, at work, at home or in life, lose passion in learning and in growing. They become resigned to where they are in life. They tire of people telling them are constantly doing things incorrectly or "wrong."

The inspired learning approach, rather than focusing on the negative, builds upon well-defined and communicated levels of competency. These competency descriptions are provided to the inspired learners allowing them to understand what it means to acquire a successful level of proficiency in the subject. In this way, learners can experiment with various approaches to learning, customized to their preferred learning modalities, all leading to the same end results.

In supporting inspired learners with only positive feedback and encouragement, facilitators are in effect acknowledging the level of competency that is demonstrated by the learners. This approach is never about lying about what's not working, but rather setting it aside. What's required is authentic, respectful communication to the learners about each success, or partial success, on the road to mastery. It acknowledges Universal Laws, especially the Law of Attraction, which states that like energies attract. Therefore attention upon the negative would create more negative. In an inspired learning environment attention to the positive creates more of that as well.

Here's a simple example. If a mother tells her daughter, "Don't spill your milk," what does the daughter have to think about to comply? Well of course, she has to think about spilling milk first. She has to picture how that would look, if she were to spill the milk. Only then can she negate the concept in her conscious mind. By then, she's already been thinking about spilling the milk. The likelihood of the young girl spilling the milk at this point is far greater than if the mother had said nothing.

Using our knowledge of the Law of Attraction, it would be more effective for the mother to state her desires in a positive way, such as, "Dear, hold on to your cup carefully as your drink your milk." It has the same intent, but allows the child to focus on the desired behavior. It allows a more supportive energy to be present and will produce more positive results. By using the Inspired Learning Model, the mother might acknowledge what she just observed when her daughter drank her milk successfully with, "Very good dear, you just drank from your cup by holding it firmly with both hands and then returned it to the table safely. Well done!" As you can see, the model celebrates successes along the way, big ones and little ones too.

There is so much more to this Model, yet I have found it so powerful in my work and my life that I wanted to introduce it briefly. To learn more about this Model and how to incorporate it into your school, your work, your home or your life, please visit the Foundation for Inspired Learning's website, at inspiredlearning.org. The Foundation provides information, training and certification for facilitators in implementing the Model. Isn't it time we bring joy, fun and celebration back into learning?

What Do I Do Next?

There's More to Learn

Life is an adventure. There's always more that you can learn. To truly master your world, you must continue in the role of learner (in addition to other roles you may play in your life). You must continue to put what you learn into action. You must master the Universal Laws and how they apply to your life. You must master many of the concepts and techniques provided in this book. However, it's not just what you learn, but how you do it. Let's look at the "how."

First, be curious. Curiosity is a key attribute to rapid learning. Wanting to know and understand how the world truly works is a natural desire. No matter what you choose to do in your life, continue learning about it. Become proficient in it. Have fun with it.

For those who want to learn at the highest levels, I recommend teaching what you know. Teaching can be done formally or informally. You may conduct a formal class or you can share what you know about specific topics (such as Universal Laws) with friends and family. People who teach what they learn experience much higher information comprehension and higher levels of retention. Therefore, becoming a teacher not only helps others but helps yourself. It allows you to experience a much deeper understanding of whatever material you teach.

Have Fun

Next, have fun. When learning is fun people want to continue to learn. For example, if you want to learn a new language then visit a country that speaks the language. Visit a neighborhood in your own community with people who speak the language and begin speaking with them at a local shop. Find recipes that are common in those countries and try them out. Eat at a restaurant that serves food from that country. Go online and meet others that want to do the same in your own community. There are many options to making anything you want to learn more fun!

Leadership and learning are
indispensible to each other.
– John F. Kennedy

Learning doesn't have to be hard. In fact, I've found that when I'm having fun, feeling safe and learning something that is interesting to me, it starts feeling easy! I have the sense that I am "learning with ease." It's not a struggle to learn the facts, try out the techniques or exercise what I've learned when I'm experiencing a sense of ease and comfort. The Inspired Learning Model, as mentioned earlier, is a powerful environment for utilizing this approach. Be gentle with yourself if you make a mistake along the way. Just learn, laugh it off, and keep going knowing that you are getting more masterful with each step you take.

Hire a Coach

All top business leaders and sports champions have coaches. Why? If they are already the best why do they need a coach? Coaches do many things, whether in sports or business. Common to all coaches is motivation. The coach supports the athlete or business professional by helping them stay focused on their goals, keeping them in motion when the inevitable bumps in the road appear, and reminding them of their ability to persevere.

Coaches provide accountability. They remind the client of what they (the client) has already determined to be most important in their life. The coach provides a gentle nudge or sometimes more, as needed to keep the goals in view and to keep moving in that direction.

(A coach) is not an advisor. He's not telling you what to do. It's more that you have capacity within yourself but you never touch these buttons. So he brings out your own capacity – or rather you discover your own capacity. You become an explorer of yourself.
– Muhammad Yunus, founder of Grameen Bank, which specializes in Micro Loans to people in developing countries; Nobel Peace Prize winner

Coaches also provide a safe environment where clients can entertain various ideas, strategies and solutions to problems in their life. Coaches are trained to actively listen and respond with direct questions that help the client get to the heart of the matter, making rapid progress toward their goals. Coaches help clients see things they are not seeing, especially at times when the client is too close to an issue and can't get the perspective to find a solution to a challenge. In short, coaches accelerate the process of creating wealth, health and success in the lives of their clients!

Are You a Tiger?

Tiger Woods, one of the world's top golfers, was interviewed about his training regimen. He was asked if he trained with his coach during the off-season. He responded that he did, for as much as 8 to 10 hours a day. Many people might wonder, why would such a successful player need to practice with his coach so much, especially during the off-season. Wasn't he satisfied with his top ranking? It would seem like he didn't need to train so much.

The truth is clear to me. It is because he chooses to continue mastering his game that he is the best in the world. He is willing to do what most people are not. He continues to improve, learn, adjust, take risks and better himself each and every time. Tiger is a true champion, not just by what he does, but by how he thinks.

No matter how good you get you can always
get better, and that's the exciting part.
– Tiger Woods

Become a Champion

Thinking from a place of possibility, continual mastery and lifelong learning is realizing that you are truly young and vibrant as long as you keep learning. Choose the people that will support you in your life. Don't "spend" money on yourself. This is called "poverty consciousness." Rather, "invest" in yourself, a viewpoint known as "prosperity consciousness." To be prosperous one must invest. The best investment you can ever make is in your own growth and learning. For many high-achievers hiring a coach is a great option to accelerate their results, and it's a great way to put all the seminars, books and CDs that you may invest in to use in your life.

Don't forget to share with others those resources, such as this book you are reading now, if they inspired you and helped you grow and succeed in life. People will be grateful for your thoughtfulness and the support of their dreams and goals!

Continue to Train

In addition to coaching, other great ways of learning and growing include reading powerful books. There is a short list of the top resources I recommend at the end of this book. I own and have read hundreds of books on leadership, personal development and peak performance. I have distilled my favorites to a single page of highly recommended titles.

Life isn't a dress rehearsal. This is it!
– Marc Carignan

Attend personal development events and seminars. Learn from the teachers who have authored many of the books on my reading list, including Anthony Robbins, James Ray and others. Listen to CDs and watch DVDs from people you connect with, trust and are interested in, whether from me and my company or other inspired teachers and mentors. Whatever you choose, follow through and read, listen, attend and put into practice what you learn.

Learn more about your life beyond the physical plane, what is usually referred to as spirituality. For many, this may include learning more about a specific religion or tradition. It may be studying western philosophies. It may be about eastern mind-body-spirit healing modalities, like energy work and acupuncture. Perhaps you have an interest in metaphysics and Universal Laws. Whatever your choose, act upon it.

Study teachers that can assist you in achieving financial wealth and prosperity. Learn the mindset of the truly wealthy, the key to financial wealth. Model those that have gone before. What works for one person will work for another.

Exercise your body. Eat healthy foods and get plenty of rest. Get fit. Your body is a temple. Wherever your go and whatever you do, you also take it with you. Take care of it and it will take care of you.

Choose to be one of the few who are designing their lives consciously. If you do what everybody does, you'll get what everybody gets. If you want more, you must make different choices in your life. Education is key to a different life.

You deserve to be successful. You deserve to be rich. It's your choice. What will you choose?

Grow and Give

You're never going to be happy by what you get. You're going to be happy by what you become. And what you become comes from how you grow and what you give.
– Anthony Robbins

I believe that there's no actual destination we need to reach in our physical existence. As much as we may love visualizing our wants and desires, and setting and accomplishing our goals, these objectives simply become mechanisms for our continued growth and ongoing experiences in life. One goal just leads to another. One desire satisfied spawns another yet to be experienced.

I've learned after great success in all areas of my life, including financially, that getting to the goal itself will never make you happy in the long term. You may enjoy reaching the goal, but most people never seem to feel that it's enough, whatever their goal was. For example, my initial goal of one million dollars sounded great, but when I achieved that goal the excitement and satisfaction quickly wore off and I wondered, "Is that what it feels like," and even, "Is that all there is?" I then went to set a new financial goal. At the time, I didn't get the underlying reason why I felt unsatisfied. Today, I know. It's about experiencing all of life, not just the financial.

I believe that setting and achieving our goals provides a pathway for us to grow and experience joy in our lives. It allows us to change and sometimes "transform" our world view in order to pursue our goals. It's really about "who" you get to be, or to become, in order to have the ability to reach your goal. It's what you had to learn, who you met and how you played the game of life on the way to the achievement of your goal. Did you work with or against people? Did you pursue goals for your benefit only or for the benefit of others as well? As you give, you shall also receive.

Life's Greatest Joys

These are the greatest joys of life: to love and be loved, to serve, to experience joy and to live life from a place of gratitude and appreciation. You truly have the power to create the life you desire. You have the ability to grow and expand. You can experience joy in any moment you choose.

Tools and techniques have been provided throughout this book to assist you in your journey. Pick one or more and begin applying them to your life. Make it fun. Make it an adventure. Are you ready?

Our greatest fear is not that we are inadequate, but that we are powerful beyond measure. It is our light, not our darkness, that frightens us. We ask ourselves, Who am I to be brilliant, gorgeous, handsome, talented and fabulous? Actually, who are you not to be? You are a child of God. Your playing small does not serve the world. There is nothing enlightened about shrinking so that other people won't feel insecure around you. We were born to make manifest the glory of God within us. It is not just in some; it is in everyone. And, as we let our own light shine, we consciously give other people permission to do the same. As we are liberated from our fear, our presence automatically liberates others.

– Marianne Williamson, from "A Course in Miracles"; also used by Nelson Mandela during his presidential inaugural address in South Africa on May 10, 1994

Leadership
Intention
Vision
Practice
Confidence
Attitude
Learning

Suggested Reading List

Awaken the Giant Within, by Anthony Robbins

Ask and It Is Given, by Esther and Jerry Hicks (The Teachings of Abraham)

The Breakthrough Experience, by John Demartini

Cashflow Quadrant, by Robert Kiyosaki

Celestine Prophecy, by James Redfield (*also on DVD*)

Confidence: Finding It And Living It, by Barbara De Angelis

Conversations with God, by Neale Donald Walsch (*also on DVD*)

Dare To Be Great, by Terry Cole-Whittaker

The Four Agreements, by Don Miguel Ruiz

Inspiration, by Wayne Dyer (*also on DVD*)

Loving What Is, by Byron Katie

Pass It On, by Scott Evans and Greg S. Reid (on DVD)

The *Positively Brilliant* Series, by Peter J. Reding (*on books and CDs*)

The Power of Focus, by Jack Canfield, Mark Victor Hansen and Les Hewitt

Power vs. Force, by David Hawkins

Practical Spirituality, by James Arthur Ray

Rays of the Dawn, by Thurman Fleet

Rich Dad, Poor Dad, by Robert Kiyosaki

The Secret, by Rhonda Byrne (*also on CD and DVD*)

The Science of Getting Rich, by Wallace D. Wattles*

The Science of Success, by James Arthur Ray

The Seven Spiritual Laws of Success, by Deepak Chopra (*also on DVD*)

The Success Principles, by Jack Canfield

Think and Grow Rich, by Napoleon Hill

Way of the Peaceful Warrior, by Dan Millman

MARC CARIGNAN

Author of "Leading from the Inside Out"
President & CEO of Life Success Strategies

MARC'S WORDS OF MOTIVATION AND INSPIRATION

Attitude is everything. Without a positive attitude, all successes are hollow and all mistakes are failures.

Be bold. Be clear. Believe in yourself.

Believe that it's possible. When you do, it is!

Do what you love, or find something you do. Life's too short to spend your time on things that don't bring you joy and happiness.

Get moving. You can't correct your course standing still.

I have a responsibility to make a difference, to use my unique set of talents and gifts.

Life isn't a dress rehearsal. This is it!

No more excuses, no more hiding out, no more doubt: just do it!

People who get what they want are committed to it and clear about it.

The purpose of relationships is to share more of who we are and in so doing become more ourselves.

You don't have to be motivated to do what you love!

You have to be different to make a difference. Otherwise you can only make a 'same-ness'!

Marc is a highly sought-after professional speaker and life coach.

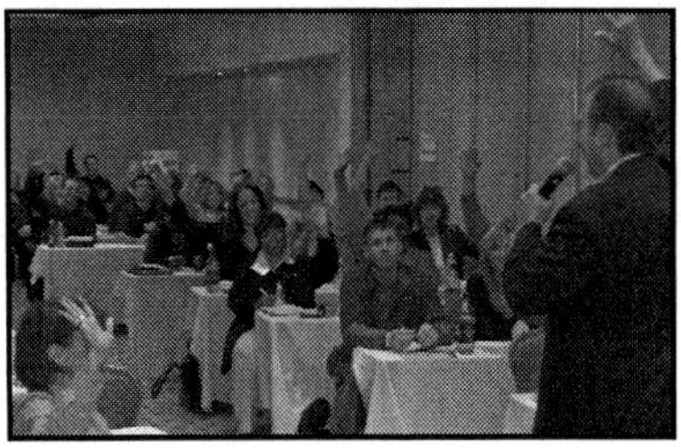

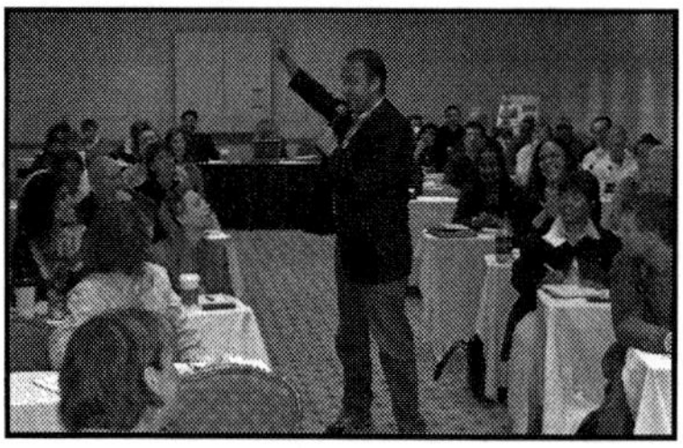

To schedule Marc for coaching for your individual or group needs, or to schedule Marc to speak at your upcoming event visit **www.LifeSuccessStrategies.com or call 1-619-299-1700.**

Are you Ready to Live the Life You Desire?

Start Living Your Life Fully Today!

BOOK NOW ON AUDIO CD

Leading from the Inside Out *(AUDIO PROGRAM)*

Are you ready to activate the power that is already within you? There's a leader within each person, even if it's not yet fully awake. This amazing, practical book provide seven steps to becoming the author of your own life, creating habits that empower and getting clear on who you truly are and what you really want. This book is a must for all who lead others as personal leadership must come first. Be a leader yourself and others will want to follow.

Special Quantity Discounts

1 Audio Program	$24.95
2-20 Audio Programs	$20.00 each
21-99 Audio Programs	$15.00 each
100-499 Audio Programs	$14.00 each
500-999 Audio Programs	$13.00 each
1000+ Audio Programs	$12.00 each

This book makes a great corporate or personal gift. To place an order visit **www.LifeSuccessStrategies.com or call 1-619-299-1700.**